The Amazing Adventures of a Midwestern Girl

BARBARA J. BARTON

DEDICATION

This collection of true short stories is dedicated to the spirit of adventure and to all those who work so hard to make the world a better place.

CONTENTS

ACKNOWLEDGMENTS

I would like to acknowledge all those who have taught me something, made me bleed, lifted me up, and rearranged my life. Life is in the journey.

Special thanks to Melanie Mack and Nicole Klarmann for editing this book.

CHAPTER 1

WESTERVILLE

Safety Patrol

When I was in early elementary school in the mid 1960's, I was selected to be on safety patrol. Now that was a huge honor. I got to have an official whistle and wear a blaze orange belt that also had a strap which went over one shoulder. These important items hung in the office on pegs and, before and after school, the safety patrol kids would race to grab their gear, sling them on, and calmly with authority walk into the hall to enforce civility among the masses.

Sometimes I was selected to be a crosswalk guard and I got to take the long wooden pole with a safety flag on the end to the crosswalk and protect all my classmates from speeding Corvairs. I would stand at attention at the edge of the road and hold the flag parallel to the ground, keeping the children behind it and safe from being squashed by a car. When traffic cleared, I walked out into the street, blocked traffic with my flag, and ushered the little kiddies to the other side of the road. I was in fourth or fifth grade at the time. Can you imagine that today? We were given so much more responsibility in those days...

One of the other major duties of safety patrol was to put up and take down the flag of the United States of America, which flew proudly from our flagpole in front of the school. And no, nobody got their tongue stuck to the pole in the winter.

It so happened I had just taken down the flag and was trying to fold it without letting it touch the ground, an offense punishable by death in those days, when I saw a naughty boy running on the sidewalk, a clear violation of the school's safety rules. I blew my whistle loudly and shouted "Hey kid, stop! No running! Stop! I said stop!" Of course, he ignored me. But what could I do? I was holding the sacred flag of the U.S. trying to keep it from touching the ground when I wasn't much taller than it was wide. I could feel my blood pressure rise. How dare he ignore a direct command from a safety patrol officer! I wadded the flag up and gave chase, but he had too much of a head start. Grumbling, I finished folding the flag and made my report to headquarters, the principal's office.

My safety patrol experience taught me many things about life. One, if given responsibility, kids stand up to the task. Two, parents in the 1960's must have been stoned to let their little children be crosswalk guards. Three, kids don't listen to other kids in positions of authority. Four, I love to be the boss. Five, that rule about not letting the flag touch the ground? It is a hindrance to carrying out law and order in the schoolyard.

Thank the good lord they don't have safety patrol these days. I can imagine kids dressed in camo with Tasers and 9mm guns furnished by the NRA. The naughty little boy that did not heed my whistle? Today he might have been toast.

I was a G.L.O.B.E. Agent

I sat in front of the old WWII radio, headphones on, listening.

"Headquarters, come in, over," I barked into the microphone. "Agent Barton here."

I turned the dials to bring the signal in better. The radio crackled. "Enemy agents have been spotted, take appropriate actions to secure top secret information."

"Roger, headquarters. I will relay to our other agents and check back in at twenty-two hundred hours," I responded. "Agent Barton, over and out."

I took off the headphones, shut down the radio, and checked my weapon. My bright green squirt gun was full, my secret agent ID was safe in my back pocket, and my spy glasses were well hidden. I carefully made my way through the cluttered garage, out the back door, and up the stairs to the second story deck. My team of agents was waiting.

"Ok, here's the deal," I said. "Headquarters has informed me that our enemies have been spotted. Our mission, should we choose to accept it, is to capture and interrogate the enemy in order to identify the location of their headquarters. Any questions?"

Paul raised his hand. "Can I go to the bathroom first?"

We were a tight knit organization called G.L.O.B.E., a name I spent hours creating. The Man from U.N.C.L.E. was my favorite TV show at the time, so to be a bona fide spy organization we had to have an acronym. I picked the name first, then went through pages of the dictionary to find the perfect words to describe our spy club. I settled on **G**ood **L**ivid **O**n **B**urly **E**spy. Sounded good to me at the time.

We posted spies behind bushes on all four corners of the house, waiting for the enemy agents to appear. It wasn't long before they were spotted, stupidly exposing themselves at the ice cream truck.

"Now!" I shouted. Our highly trained G.L.O.B.E. agents descended on the ice cream truck in a flash and managed to capture one of the enemy agents. We took the unwilling captive to our top-secret headquarters in the garage, an empty space behind a stack of boxes. I put the headphones on and contacted the higher ups once more.

"Agent Barton here, we have captured an enemy agent and will begin questioning." They were pleased.

We interrogated our prisoner for several minutes, trying to find out what top secret information he had. But we were interrupted by shouts and screams from our guards outside the garage door.

"It's Brownie, RUN!"

Oh no, not Brownie! The neighbor's giant six-foot tall blonde Great Dane was known to have bitten every kid on the block at least once. I still have a scar on my hip where Brownie sunk his teeth into me one fine day. The only way to avoid him was to carry pieces of meat with you at all times. When Brownie came running at you, all you could do was throw the meat as far as you could then run like hell.

We released our prisoner and began our race home, trying to avoid the giant Great Dane that seemed to delight in terrorizing the neighborhood kids. Brownie ran after one kid then spun around and chased several more. Finally, he trotted home, satisfied he had given us a fright. Fortunately, every one made it to safety before becoming Brownie's Saturday afternoon snack.

I slipped back in to headquarters and once again put on the headphones. "Headquarters, this is Agent Barton," I said, trying to catch my breath. "We have lost our prisoner due to an attack by a six-foot tall Great Dane. Will resume search tomorrow."

"Roger, Agent Barton. Over and out."

I grabbed a hot dog out of the garage refrigerator and warily made my way home, prepared for the flash of blond waiting to dart out of the bushes and consume me.

Light as a Feather Stiff as a Board

I don't know about you, but my childhood was filled with wonder. I had a magic set and held captivating and mysterious shows in our basement. The trick I remember most was the disappearing ball. There was this blue plastic vase-shaped thing, with what looked like a plastic ball sitting in it. In all actuality it was simply a secondary lid that looked like a ball. I lifted the real top off the plastic vase-shaped thing and said, "Look at the ball! Now, I will make it disappear!" I would put the top back on and lift it off again, this time taking the fake plastic ball up with it. The outer edges of the most magnificent magical prop were ribbed, so no one could tell I had an extra piece.

"Ooooohhhhh. Ahhhhhhhhh!" the crowd would exclaim, then break into thunderous applause.

Another ghoulish trick I read about in a magic book always drove my Mom crazy. I would innocently walk up to her with a small white box in my hand, you know the kind of box I mean. Palm sized, the one you usually get a necklace in if you buy it at Sears or something. Anyway, I would hand her the box and say "Open it!" She would smile and take the lid off and inside would be a severed finger covered in blood. Mom would fall for this every time. She would jump a startled kind of jump and then say in her Mom voice, "Barbara Jean!" I would burst out laughing. The magic book said to cut a hole in the bottom of the box just big enough for your middle finger to fit through. Then, hold the box in your hand with your finger laying nicely on the bottom of the box. Stuff some cotton balls around it and strategically place bright red ketchup on the finger. And there you have it, a severed finger. It's a wonder Mom still talks to me.

I played with Ouija Boards, held séances, read tea leaves. But nothing compared to Light as a Feather Stiff as a Board. After a little research, I found that this "game" was played as far back as the seventeenth century during the plague in London. Here's how we did it. One person would lay on the floor. Usually we had five to six kids who would sit cross-legged around the body, one at the head, two on each side, and one at the feet. Each kid would place two fingers from each hand under the body. The person seated at the head (me of course) would tell a tale of how the poor soul died, usually by some fatal car crash. Then we would chant; "She's dying," I would say. "She's dying," they would repeat. "She's dead," I would say. "She's dead," they would chant. "She's as light as a feather." "She's as light as a feather." "She's as stiff as a board." "She's as stiff as a board."

"Let us lift her to her grave." "Let us lift her to her grave." "Lift," I would command.

You could hear a pin drop, no, you could hear a hair drop the air was so still. Slowly, we would lift the body into the air, levitating our "dead" friend as high as we could. Then, just as slowly, we would lower her to the ground.

Wikipedia's explanation of this phenomenon is that when you have several people lifting a heavy object, the weight is distributed evenly and it is totally possible to lift a body. I would agree with that if each person was using their arms and hands fully. But only four fingers?

One night we asked one of the Mom's to be our "dead body". She happily obliged. We went through the ritual and lifted her up above the floor a good two feet. Easily. Someone giggled and broke the spell. We dropped her.

Now to all you non-believers, doubting Thomas', cynics, and skeptics, I am here to tell you that we lifted this woman as though she truly was as light as a feather. There is no way under the sun you can lift twenty pounds with your index and middle fingers alone as though it was a piece of paper.

Seems to me I tried Light as a Feather Stiff as a Board as an adult at some point in my life. It didn't work. Perhaps it was because the rest of the participants were non-believers. Perhaps our "dead body" wore a plus size. Perhaps it is because there is some truth that children are more open to other worlds, not yet jaded. The reason matters not to me. I am a believer.

CHAPTER 2

EDWARDSBURG

The Pig Farmer and the Crypt

Back behind a house I once lived in was an old field. And in that old field were my fort, a creek, and a well-worn trail winding through the adjacent woods into the cemetery. This old cemetery sat on high ground, with steep slopes on its edges worn by erosion and curious kids. The cemetery introduced itself to travelers on this particular trail by presenting a mysterious crypt, guarded by rusty, heavy metal doors that creaked when opened. I remember the first time I discovered that crypt. With only the light of the sun shining through the cracked doorway, I peered inside. There were steel beams arranged in racks, a dirt floor, and ceiling and walls dotted with inscriptions from previous explorers. I gathered my courage and entered, mesmerized by what I was sure was the archaeological discovery of the century. The smell of cool damp soil and aging metal filled my nostrils. What was this place? The signatures on the walls and ceiling dated back over fifty years. I was in heaven.

It was during this time my middle sister was dating the son of a

8

pig farmer, let's call him Bobby B. Bobby B. had red hair, freckles, was a bit stocky, and wore bib overalls as standard garb. He was also what one might call full of machismo.

One day I decided to assist Bobby B. in getting in touch with his feminine side. I told him of this dark, scary crypt that I had discovered but was too afraid to enter. Would he go and protect me? "Of course," he said in a manly sort of way.

So, the date was set for that Friday night. In the dark.

Friday afternoon I hopped on my bike and rode to the town's only grocery store to spend my Tastee Freeze earnings on several packages of raw liver and fishing line. I then road back across town to my street, then turned east and peddled my bike a quarter mile to the proper entrance of the cemetery. I ditched my ten speed next to the old tombstone with the angel on top and slid down the hill to the entrance of the crypt.

Carefully I removed the liver from its packaging and threaded several strands of fishing line through the juiciest pieces. Slowly and deliberately I began to make my way around the crypt, strategically placing chunks of cold organ on ledges where one would be mostly likely to place an unsuspecting hand. I hung liver décor in areas sure to draw attention. It was a masterpiece.

Later that night me, Bobby B., my sister, and a few other friends gathered at our home on Hamilton Street, readying ourselves for the trip. Flashlights? Check. Candy bars? Check. Cans of pop? Check. "Are you sure you want to do this?" I asked the group, fabulously feigning fright. Bobby B. assured us there was nothing to fear as long as he was with us.

We started down the trail, five lanky teens and Bobby B., with beams of light bouncing off tall grasses and trees. "Are you guys sure you want to do this?" I again asked, this time exuding so much fear I almost had myself convinced. "Aw come on you chickens!" said the pig farmer's son. "Only if you go first Bobby B," I said. So, he did.

Old green pots with faded plastic flowers began to appear, signaling that we were getting close to the crypt. Bobby B. began to slow. "What's the matter Bobby B.?" I asked? "Nothing!" he sort of bravely shouted. "It's in there, behind that old rusty door," I said. "What was this place for?" someone asked. "I was told this is where they stored dead bodies in the winter, when the ground was too frozen to dig. That is why there are racks in there, they piled up the caskets all the way to the ceiling," I informed them. Bobby B.'s expression began to change. Was that worry? Fear?

"Go on Bobby B., you go in first."

Bobby B. slowly opened the door, its rusty hinges adding to the ambience of the evening. He entered the musty room and began to make his way around the crypt, the others followed. Except me. Soon I heard a scream, no a squeal, no maybe it was best described as a squeam. Then, a great commotion ensued and Bobby B. burst through the doorway of the old crypt screaming better than a girl. I never knew someone could run so fast in bib overalls. I laughed in hysterics as Bobby B. disappeared down the trail, still emitting sounds of great terror. Close behind were the rest of kids. Me? I sat down and laughed so hard I cried.

Bobby B. never dated my sister again. I hope she forgives me.

Detasseling - A Midwestern Rite of Passage

Driving through the countryside today, I watched as the Imperial Crop Walkers made their way through the fields detasseling corn. Straight out of Star Wars, these large mechanical monstrosities have giant tires that lift the guts of the beast above the corn plants, allowing their jaws of death to rip the tassels from the poor lowly corn plants below.

According to Wikipedia, detasseling corn is the process of removing the pollen-producing flowers (the tassel) from the tops of the corn plants and placing them on the ground. It is a form of pollination control employed to cross-breed, or hybridize, two varieties of corn.

Back when I was a kid, we did this. By "we" I mean the teen workforce in our village. It was hot, dirty work I was told (I had opted for a trailer factory job) and one that was not on the top ten list of best places to work (which is why I opted for said trailer factory job). But I know that the kids who went to the fields grew up knowing what a hard day's work was all about. It was a rite of passage.

But then came the Crop Walkers.

Developed in the 1970's (when I was a teenager), the machines replaced the teens. Apparently, it was becoming more difficult to convince the restless youth to spend their summers in the corn fields, so with a dwindling teen work force, the Crop Walkers were created. Necessity is the mother of invention so they say.

The Imperial Crop Walkers are not able to detassel all the corn so there are still human beings required to finish the job. Some are teens, but nowadays most are migrant workers.

I have a hunch that the increase in rabble rousing among the younger sector of our population may somehow be tied to the disappearance of the teen detasseling rite of passage. All a teen could do after working in the corn fields was eat and sleep. So, I vote for calling in Luke Skywalker, Princess Leah, Chewy, and

Hans Solo and have them blast the Imperial Crop Walkers to smithereens. Let the young folks build some character and muscles out in the fields again. Then, in twenty or thirty years when they are the leaders of this land, they will remember what a hard day's work all about is.

The Autograph Book

Grandma Belle and Grandpa Roy lived next door in an old white house with a big mulberry tree next to it. Grandma Belle always made me a mulberry pie if I would pick the berries for her. Oh, that was delicious. Grandpa Roy was the official umpire of our kickball games over at the Grover's. The elderly couple were much loved in our neighborhood.

Behind their old white house was a big red barn with vines and moss attaching themselves to its sturdy wood, as if holding on for dear life. To go into that old barn was to step back in time. There were stacks of old newspapers telling of the bombing of Hiroshima and the assassination of JFK. An old black top hat rested on a stack of newsprint and found itself on the head of every kid who snuck in for a visit. There were boxes of clothes and old household items. And amongst the heaps and mounds, a velvet covered autograph book with real autographs inside. This treasure I kept.

Every night I would carefully open the old book and touch the pages, each with the fancy signature of a person unknown to me. The writing style was of the old days when people took pride in their penmanship, and it was clear they were written with quill or cartridge pens. I wondered about each person, who they were, where they lived. Were they famous or just a friend? Questions that would never have answers.

I have always been an autograph hound, not a serious one, but I have acquired my share of famous signatures. The first autograph I got was from Bart Starr, quarterback of the Green Bay Packers in the 1960s. I wrote him a letter and asked for a picture and sure enough one came in the mail, signed by the famous quarterback himself. Next, I wrote to the Monkees and soon an autographed picture was in the mailbox with all four signatures from the famous primates. On a roll, I sent a Christmas card to President and Lady Bird Johnson. They sent one back.

In the early 1980s, I went to the Wizard of Oz Convention and found myself staring at three, not one, but three living, breathing

Munchkins! It took me an hour to collect myself in order to go speak to them. They were REAL! I mean, one of them was the Coroner for God's sake, the one who examined the Wicked Witch of the West and found she was really most sincerely dead! I had watched the Munchkins every year since the day I was born and, well, it was like seeing the real Santa Claus. I left the Wizard of Oz Convention that day with three Munchkin autographs.

My next autograph extravaganza occurred on a leather guitar strap that I took with me to gigs where I shared the stage with other performers. I would ask my fellow musicians to sign that strap and I am pleased to say it is full of signatures from most of my favorite folk musicians. What great memories that strap holds.

I did send away for...OK paid for an autograph from Xena Warrior Princess (Lucy Lawless). I couldn't help myself. I was going through my Xena phase.

I bought a book once that told which movie stars would respond to autograph requests. So, when my Grandma was still suffering the blues from losing my Grandpa, I decided to cheer her up by writing to her favorite TV character (next to Xena and Zorro), Walker Texas Ranger, played by Chuck Norris. He was one of the actors the book said would write back. I told him how Grandma was one of his biggest fans, and that she was still sad about losing Grandpa. I asked if he might send her an autographed picture to cheer her up.

About six months later, Grandma got her picture. A personalized autograph to Phyliss Barton from Chuck Norris, aka Walker Texas Ranger. I was so excited! He really did respond. I was sure she would feel better.

She chuckled a suspicious chuckle, a kind of "huh huh" thing, and proclaimed, "That's not real, I am sure his secretary signed it."

When Grandma died, I stuck Chuck's picture in her casket along with her and Grandpa's well-worn deck of cards and a scribbled scoresheet (he owed her), and some Yahtzee dice. I was sure that the autograph verifier in heaven would confirm to Grandma that this was indeed a real autograph.

My last autograph came from President Barack Obama, a hand-written postcard addressed to me and delivered Priority Mail. In it, he told me that although sometimes slowly, America marches toward equality and freedom. He responded to an email I had sent months earlier, thanking him for supporting civil rights for gays and lesbians. I can only hope my letter had a tiny bit of influence in his support of same-sex marriage.

But these autographs aren't the ones that mean the most to me. I treasure the autographs nestled in the signed cards or letters from those I love. These are the priceless pages I hold dear, written without prompting or payment. Professions of love.

The Race Horse Ranch

Lately I have had a hankering for a hat. I guess I was first inspired from watching Dr. Quinn Medicine Woman reruns. She had the absolutely coolest hats. Of course, I researched these fine-crafted head coverings and found out they were custom made by a famous hat maker named Jack Kellogg at Hatman Jack's. Figures. But ever tenacious, I have been searching high and low for a hat like she wore to no avail. So yesterday on my way home, I stopped at Tom's Western Wear in Ovid to see if I could find my dream hat. After all, it was my Birth Day, so lady luck should be with me, right?

The minute I opened the door and stepped into that store, I instantly transformed from a newly hatched 54-year-old to an innocent, spirited girl of 13. My eyes grew wide as they traveled from left to right around this very large shop, gazing at bridles and harnesses and shiny sterling silver belt buckles. I was in heaven.

"Can I help you?" asked the first of several western wear-attired clerks I encountered during my visit. "No, thanks, I am just browsing," I lied. I was there for a hat. MY hat. But I was a bit shy for some reason, so I feigned disinterest and continued my slow walk toward the hat department. It was when I entered the saddle room that I left my body and traveled back in time to Edwardsburg.

Down the street from our house was a race horse ranch, with over two hundred fifty acres of woods and fields, a track with two starting gates, three stables, a round swimming pool for training, and a tack room. I don't recall how I met the owner, Mr. Kling, but one summer I lived a dream.

Mr. Kling taught me how to feed and water the horses, clean the stalls, rub liniment on their legs and bandage them, put them on the walker, swim them, brush them down, and saddle and bridle them. But the best thing I learned was how to drive a tractor. I could hitch up the manure spreader, back it into the barns, load it up, and then drive it out into the fields where I spread the wonderful smelling dung. I also learned to drag the racetrack, which made it as smooth as a baby's butt. All this and I was only 13 years old.

My friends Kim and Kay had a part Arabian/part Quarter horse named Kiko, and sometimes we would go riding together at the ranch. Mr. Kling would let me take one of the stable horses, usually a pony horse (one used to lead the race horses). One day Kim and I went up to the race track. Mr. Kling always warned us to never put the horses in the starting gates. So, we put the horses in the starting gates. "Go!" I shouted, and we were off. Both horses burst from the gates and ran full speed, hooves and sand flying, and two young girls having the thrill of their lives. Soon, however, that thrill turned into momentary terror as we lost control of the large animals. We were no longer racing each other, they were. It was then I learned why race horses wear blinders.

"Whoa, whoa, WHOA!" we yelled at the horses, holding on for dear life. As they made their way around the turn I was sure I would roll off the horse and into the weeds, but by some miracle I held on. After what seemed like eternity, the horses ran out of steam and began to slow down. When we finally got them stopped, we jumped off and took a few minutes to calm our wildly beating hearts. Wow. What a ride. That was a secret we never told Mr. Kling, although I am sure the next time he went out to train a horse on the track, the record of our race was well kept in the sand.

One day while I was hanging out in the tack room reading old issues of Quarter Horse Journal, Mr. Kling brought in a pair of well-worn brown cowboy boots. "Here," he said, handing me the boots. "For you." I took those boots home, shined them up right pretty, and put them on. My first pair of real cowboy boots. Of course, they were several sizes too big but I didn't care. I put on two pairs of socks, pulled the boots on, and walked all the way back to the ranch, proudly strutting my shiny new boots.

Once, Mr. Kling went out of town for a weekend and asked me if

I would be in charge of the ranch while he was away. I was to feed, water, and walk the horses, clean the stalls, and keep an eye on things. He also instructed me to take the tractor and load the manure in the spreader and take it out to the fields. Quite a bit of responsibility for such a young girl, but I eagerly accepted.

My first day taking care of the ranch in my brown cowboy boots was awesome. I backed the tractor into the barn with no problem and cleaned all the stalls, filling the manure spreader. It was when I got to the prize stallion's stall that the trouble began. This horse, named Right Turn, was not a happy horse. He was always kicking the stall and had a look in his eye that made me not trust him. As soon as I opened his stall door, he bolted and knocked me out of the way and ran out into the barn. "Oh shit!" was all I could say. I ran and closed the barn door, and there we were. Me and him. It was show down time. I tried my best to get that damn horse back in the stall but he would have none of it. So, after much cerebral ruminating, I figured the only thing I could do was put a bucket of oats in his stall and hope that his love of food was greater than his desire to bust out of the barn. It worked.

Mr. Kling came home from his trip and was very happy that I had taken such good care of the ranch. Everything was spic and span, the horses were well, the stalls were clean, I even cleaned up the tack room. Mr. Kling took me down to the local diner and bought me a cup of coffee and a big piece of cherry pie. I sat there in my brown cowboy boots, sipping my black coffee and eating pie just like I was in Dodge City. I loved my life.

"Can I help you?" another western wear clad clerk asked, snapping me out of my daydream. "You already have," I replied.

The Golf Ball War

My mom and dad were golfers when I was growing up. Dad still hits the back nine every once in a while. They even convinced me to take golf lessons. I had a set of aquamarine stained woods and the usual clobber clubs. Just wasn't my thing. But they seemed to love it.

I preferred to use golf balls for something to bounce. Before the Super Ball came on the market, golf balls were queen. They made a sound like a ping pong ball when they hit the pavement and bounced as high as the clouds. You could walk along bouncing a golf ball just like a basketball, but they had a mind of their own and were much trickier to catch.

Ever curious, I began to wonder just what was inside a golf ball that made them bounce. It must be something very powerful because it can bounce really high even though it has a shell around the bounce material. So, I asked my Dad.

"Tightly wound rubber bands," he answered. That made sense to me, rubber bounces right?

One afternoon the Grover kids were sitting on Grandma and Grandpa Roy's porch with me and my sisters and the subject of golf balls came up. "My Dad said golf balls bounce because they have tightly wound rubber bands in them," I proclaimed, a thirteen-year-old know-it-all. "Well, MY Dad says they bounce because they have a hard rubber center!" challenged one of the Grovers. "Nuh-uh," I said. "Uh-huh," he said.

"Nuh-uh." "Uh-huh." "Nuh-uh!" "Uh-huh!"

The line was drawn. The Golf Ball War was on.

The Grovers stomped off to their house across the street, the Bartons stomped off to their house next door. Tempers were high. Faces had scowls.

The first thing I did was to write a protest song. John Lennon's

"Power to the People" was a hit then and fit nicely for my cause. I simply changed the lyrics to "Power to the Bartons". We went back to Grandma and Grandpa Roy's porch and began to sing.

We kids didn't speak much for the next few weeks, each standing their ground on this most important kid issue. But after a while I started to miss playing with my friends across the street. A truce was drawn and a golf ball was sawed open. Rigid rubber core, rubber band lining.

The Golf Ball War lasted two weeks. It wasn't about the golf balls, really. It was about loyalty to our families and what we believed to be true. It was also about the inability of children to understand there are different points of view and to accept others beliefs even if they are different from our own. And it also shows how blind faith can bite you in the butt.

You would think we would have learned something since then.

Winstons

In our first house on Hamilton Street we had a basement which was divided into two rooms. In room one was an unfinished something or another, perhaps a bench or maybe a planter. Visualize a two-feet by five-feet wall of bricks that make a sharp right turn, stacked up maybe two feet tall. The perfect hiding place for something small.

I attended junior high school then and was a relatively good kid, unlike the "hoods" we would see walking down the street in our small town, smoking cigarettes and saying naughty words. No, I wasn't like THEM. During lunchtime, the hoods would race out to Smoky Oaks, the forbidden woods next to the school, and smoke their cigarettes and do other unspeakable things. The buzzer would ring and you could watch them sprint across the big field, trying to catch their smoky breaths as they hurried to get to fifth period.

This was the 1970s. Post hippie. That confused time between the groovy bell-bottomed, love-beaded, and velvet-chokered sixties and the sweet mullet-headed, glam band era of the eighties. I mean, where do you go after a generation of free love, what is left to discover? For me, it was Winstons.

Why is it that a TV jingle can stick in your mind for decades? I can sing you every cigarette commercial since 1958.

"Come out for the Kooooooool taste, the Koolest pleasure every time you smoke."

"You can take Salem out of the country BUT, you can't take the country out of Salem."

"Winston tastes good like a [uh uh] cigarette should."

It was this last one that got me. Cigarettes looked like they tasted good, my Mom and Dad smoked them (Virginia Slims, Kools, Salem), the Marlboro Man smoked them while riding horses, and the hoods sucked them down like I did Slo Pokes. So, when I decided one fall day to try these delicious white sticks of tobacco, there was no hesitation. I would smoke the best tasting cigarette in the world. Winstons. Now, how to get a pack. Fortunately for me, just one block away was a gas station usually staffed by only one man. Whenever a customer pulled up and the bell rang, he would grab his red mechanics rag, wipe his hands, and walk out to greet his visitor. "Can I check your oil today?" he would ask. He would put the nozzle into the car, lift the hood, and check the oil. Then, he would drop the hood and clean the windshield until it sparkled. The customer would pay him, he would reach into his navy blue, oil stained trousers and pull out a wad of crumbled up bills, and give them their change. A wave goodbye, and he went back into the station to his cup of coffee, cigarette, and newspaper.

The time from wiping hands to the wave goodbye - five minutes, twenty-three seconds average. Plenty of time for this tow-headed neighbor kid to put forty-five cents of her paper route money into the cigarette machine, pull the shiny silver knob, and watch her brand new pack of Winstons drop to the bottom. Push open flap, grab, and place in pocket. Wait for man to start his return into station. Put another ten cents of paper route money into candy machine, pull shiny silver knob for a Payday, and watch it drop to bottom. Push open flap, grab, tear open wrapper, and eat candy bar loudly to squelch suspicion. Cheerfully say thanks and walk inconspicuously home. Mission accomplished.

Now, where to hide my brand new pack of Winstons. I had two snoopy little sisters, and two snoopy big parents. I know, the brick thingymajigger in the basement! I nonchalantly went downstairs, lifted out a few bricks here and moved a few bricks there, creating a nice little hiding spot. In went the Wintons. Tomorrow would be the day I smoked my first cigarette.

I arose earlier than the rest of the family, and sneaked downstairs to retrieve my new pack of Winstons. I stuck them deep in my coat pocket, ate my breakfast, and headed off to school which was a good mile away.

Damn, it was harder than I thought, sneaking a smoke on my way to school. Cars kept passing me. My town only had nine hundred people in it, so everybody knew everybody. "There is Barb Barton!" I could imagine them saying. "Look, honey, is that a CIGARETTE she is smoking?" "My word!" Then my Mom and Dad would get a call and I would be grounded for at least two weeks, if not more. But I had no choice. That jingle was playing over and over in my head. "Winston tastes good like a cigarette should."

I made my move. I pulled the brand new pack of Winstons from my coat pocket, took off my mittens, and opened it. Tap, tap, tap just like my Dad did. Why do people do that? Anyway, I pulled out my cigarette, put it in my mouth and lit it, hiding all the while behind my very large mittens. Car! Oh, what is that on the ground over there? I pretend to pick up something. They don't suspect. I am safe. I held the cigarette between my lips while putting my mittens back on, then inhaled. The world spinned. I felt, I felt, I felt...dizzy. I coughed. I puked. Winston's didn't taste good, they tasted horrible! What was that commercial talking about?

On my way home from school that day I stopped by the gas station and tossed my Winstons into the trash with the used blue paper towels, empty oil containers, and cigarette butts. I put 10 cents of my paper route money into the pop machine and pushed the button for a Dr. Pepper. I popped the top, tossed the metal ring into the trash next to the Winstons, and walked home, singing, "Dr. Pepper, so misunderstood, if everyone would try one they would know it tastes good!"

The Case of the Missing Keys

My parents were good friends with Del Shannon's sister Blanche. In fact, there is a rumor that he actually babysat us kids once or twice, though my Father now says that is hooey. I remember visiting Blanche and family at their home near Muskegon and gazing in awe at the Del Shannon albums on the wall, a tribute to her famous brother.

One summer, Blanche and her family came to visit us in Edwardsburg. I am sure the menfolk were off working on snowmobile engines or some such thing. I overheard Blanche and my mom were trying to think of something to do with the kids. "I have an idea!" I offered with enthusiasm. "Let's all go down to the cemetery and look at the gravestones." "In the dark," I added. After some discussion, all agreed that would be a fun thing to do.

After a supper of goulash and tater tots, we piled in the white Chrysler station wagon with the fake wood panels on the side, Mom driving and Blanche in the passenger seat. All six of us kids crammed in the back, half of us behind them and the rest in that weird seat that faced backwards in the rear of the car – the seat that always made you carsick if you were the unfortunate soul sentenced to sit there.

We backed out of the driveway and headed off a quarter mile east to the old cemetery road. A left turn placed us on the soft sandy dirt drive that had a strip of green grass growing down the middle. We passed by the entrance sign and pulled up to a stop at the top of the hill. It was dark, real dark. I had filled Mom and Blanche's heads full of stories about unusual headstones in the cemetery, the crypt, and added a few local tales of terror such as the glowing tombstone, gravity hill, and the Mullen Road Monsters for good measure earlier that day. I wanted to be sure they had a quality experience.

Car doors popped open and out we spilled into the cemetery's darkness. Everyone except me that is. I couldn't help but notice

Mom had left the keys in the ignition. Poor Mom. I took my time getting out of the car, and as stealthily as a ninja, snatched the keys and put them in my pocket. The stage was set.

I led the nighttime tour of the cemetery, visiting the unusual headstones and peering over the edge of the embankment to get a glimpse of the crypt (they were too scared to go near it). Then the discussion turned to ghosts and goblins. I told them of the cemetery on the way to Dowagiac where you could see a glowing tombstone as you entered, but which would mysteriously disappear when you tried to find it. The tension began to rise, the fear was so thick in the air you could taste it. Soon, it was no longer bearable. Mom and Blanche and all the kids ran screaming back to the car and jumped in, half-laughing and half-crying, literally in hysterics. They wanted out of there NOW. When the last car door shut, Mom reached for the keys. Gone! "Where are the keys, where are the keys!" she screamed frantically. Poor Blanche was so shaken she peed her pants. Literally. Thank god for vinyl seats.

As you might imagine, I could contain myself no longer. My giggles erupted into laughter, which became contagious once the rest of the kids caught on. I handed the keys to Mom and I believe she burned rubber on that dirt driveway, throwing stones and dirt one hundred yards behind her. She never did go back to that cemetery. I believe I shared the doghouse with FiFi that night.

The Mullen Road Monsters

Every small town has its legends. Ours was no different. Here, then, is the tale of the Mullen Road Monsters.

Way out in the country, down a long dirt road, is a swamp. This swamp is not unlike any other swamp, with one exception. It is the home to the Mullen Road Monsters, seven feet tall, hairy beasts that have remained undetected for hundreds, maybe thousands of years. Undetected, except by the locals who have seen the evidence, caught a glimpse, felt the fear.

If you have read my other stories, you know that I HAD to investigate these creatures, to see for myself if they did indeed exist. Call me the Fox Mulder of the seventies. I had no fear. Well, except for looking in the mirror in the bathroom in the dark and repeating "I don't believe in Miss Marysworth, I don't believe in Miss Marysworth, I don't believe in Miss Marysworth". That, my friends, is another story for another time.

I decided to travel out into the country to find Mullen Road and verify the reports I had collected from my peers, other small town residents, and the Ouija board. It seems there was a house trailer located at the edge of the swamp that had been visited by the Mullen Road Monsters. Their 1960's Volkswagen Beetle had been picked up, taken to the far end of their circle drive, and turned upside down. As if that wasn't bad enough, the Monsters had also pummeled the side of the trailer with their fists.

A second report stated that every home located in the area had large street lights strategically placed in their yards, apparently to scare off the Monsters in the dark.

The third piece of information, which led me to believe in conspiracy theories, was that every resident around the swamp had taken photographs of these secretive beasts, but that the United States Air Force had come in and confiscated them all. This was most intriguing to me.

As the Mullen Road Monsters were known only to come out at night, I had no choice but to travel into the darkness one small town Saturday night. With one friend to witness what I hoped would be verification of these distant cousins of Bigfoot, we jumped into my Chevy Camaro and headed north into the backwoods and swamps of Southwest Michigan.

I turned down Mullen Road, gravel crunching under the tires. Off in the distance I could see street lights glowing from the edges of the swamp. It wasn't long before there appeared on the right a house trailer with a circle drive. And big dents all over the side of it, the size of large fists. And at the end of the drive, a Volkswagen Beetle. I took a big gulp.

Slowly my tan Camaro crept down the long hill, approaching the swamp. The old dirt road had been put down right smack through the center of it many years before. Maybe that is why the Mullen Road Monsters were a bit unhappy. Anyway, I let the car roll in neutral to a natural stopping point, pushed in the knobs that extinguished the headlights, and turned off the engine. We waited.

Now unless you have had the experience of sitting in the middle of a swamp in the middle of a moonlit night in the middle of nowhere with nothing but your paranoid thoughts to keep you company, you may not be able to appreciate the level of fear that seeped into our hearts. I never really stopped to think about what we would do if that seven-foot tall hairy beast appeared, perhaps to tip my Camaro over with us in it. But I was determined to once and for all put some truth to the stories of the Mullen Road Monsters.

Twenty-eight long minutes passed with nothing but the sound of frogs drifting from the swamp. Then they stopped. Just like that. Silence. We went on high alert.

Somewhere in the swamp I heard a twig snap, a rustle in the bushes, a splash. Then silence.

Were they watching us? Were they about to pick the Camaro up by the rear bumper and run it into the deep muck, where we would never be heard from again? I began to tremble, I began to shake, and I could take it no more. I started the Camaro up, shoved it into first, and threw dirt as we barreled down that old country road faster than a flea on a dog's belly.

The next morning, I inspected my car. There, on the back fender, was a muddy hand print and a strand of long, brown hair.

I never went down that road again.

CHAPTER 3

FAMILY

Herman

I opened my refrigerator this morning and Herman, my Grandmother's sourdough starter, had a temper tantrum and erupted over the sides of his dough house (glass jar). Luckily, he maintained some self-control and did not explode all over the inside of the fridge as he has done before. He gets attached to some of his fridge neighbors and doesn't deal well when they get, well, eaten up. Poor Herman is the only fridge resident that never moves on, and I think it gets to him every once in a while.

Herman was gifted to my Grandmother back in 1982 from a friend of hers in Florida. Grandma fed Herman weekly up until her death in 2005. Then I became Herman's human. It is a huge responsibility you know. What if I forget to feed Herman and he, um, expires? Oh, the guilt and shame I would feel! I have grown very fond of Herman. I can see why Grandma took care of him for so very long. He truly has personality, you can tell his moods by his consistency. Some days he is very thick headed, others he is thin-doughed and you have to be careful about hurting his feelings. Some days he sweats (even in the fridge!). Then there are those days he blows his top (literally). But all in all, we have a good steady relationship, much better than I have with some humans in fact!

Every once in a while, if I don't create something with Herman, he gets fat and is too big for his dough-house. Like now. So, I can either make some sourdough bread or coffeecake, or put him in a bigger dough-house and let him keep getting fat. Now that would help keep ME from getting bigger.

I have spoken with Herman and asked if he would like to share himself with some of my friends. At first, he felt a bit torn apart by the thought, but then said that it might be cool to see other refrigerators around the Great Lakes (he has only been to Bonita Springs, Florida, Angola, Indiana, and Lansing Michigan, and a brief trip to Montrose Michigan, but that part of him expired due to neglect...we won't get into that, the therapy bills were astronomical!). Anyway, if you would like to have a cup of Herman to start your own Herman adventures, let me know and I will fatten him up before our next get together. He comes complete with instructions from Grandma. You will need to bring a mason jar to take him home in. Oh, I am getting teary-eyed at the thought!

Grandpa's Silent Night

The fireplace was beautiful. A large ten-foot wooden plank topped a wall of rounded field stones. My Grandpa built that fireplace. Twinkling lights, statues, bowling trophies, and angels decorated the mantel. The wood crackled and snapped as the fire roared, the sweet smell of smoke lightly scenting the room. The fireplace was part of our family, always lit when we gathered together at my Grandparent's home in the woods.

The room was full of family, cousins and second cousins, parents and grandparents, aunts and uncles. Our voices united as we sang Christmas carols along with Grandma's old player piano, a ritual that has lasted for years. "Get your guitar out Barbie!" someone would say. So, I would pull out my guitar and let the piano take a rest. A rousing version of Jingle Bells would ensue.

My Grandpa Barton was a mechanical engineer and college professor who swore he couldn't carry a tune. That fact was confirmed by many members of the family. But I found out it was a lie.

At the last Christmas celebration of his life, the family was once again together, singing songs of the holiday. I was seated right next to the fire and Grandpa was on the foot stool directly in front of me.

"What do you want to sing next?' I asked. Grandpa said, "Silent Night." And so, we began.

I had to lean forward a bit and tilt my head to hear, but Grandpa was singing. Softly, tenderly. It was the voice of an angel. The most beautiful version of Silent Night I have ever heard. His pale blue eyes framed by raised eyebrows gave a look of extreme sincerity, as though he were singing to baby Jesus himself. Tears welled up in my eyes. My Grandpa passed away in the fall of the following year, but he left me with a memory I will never forget. When I sing Silent Night, I see and hear him sweetly singing right along with me. Merry Christmas Grandpa.

31

Safeguard

When I was quite young, my favorite place in the world was in Grandma Barton's bath tub. The soft colors and carpet were soothing and quiet. In the corner of the tub was a plastic turtle soap dish, and I loved to put the turtle in the water and make it swim, much like a rubber ducky. Except the turtle could dive, unlike those fat yellow ducks.

In that turtle soap dish was a bar of Safeguard. And in that bathtub, I felt safer than anywhere else in the world.

When we are young, our worlds are no larger than the dappled sunlight on the sidewalk, the crickets in our backyards, the little red berries on the bushes around the house (don't eat them or you'll die!). We did not know of rape and murder, suicide and war, brutality and abuse. At least most of us didn't. Our eyes were wide open with wonder at all the magic of this big new world we had burst into.

In Grandma's tub, I was at peace. I was covered in suds and splashing and laughing and slippery as heck. I didn't know it at the time, but in every second of my bliss the scent of Safeguard was entering my little nose, imprinting on my brain.

As the years traveled on, sometimes Irish Spring took the place of Safeguard in Grandma's soap dish. It didn't have the same effect on me. All I could hear in my head was that darn commercial, "Irish Spring...manly yes, but I like it too!"

Luckily, Safeguard outlasted Irish Spring and right up until Grandma's last days on Earth, her bathroom was filled with that wonderful calming scent.

Some days life is hard. Real hard. I long for those simpler times, when all I cared about were frogs and dappled sunlight and fireflies. I don't want to know the things I know, or see the things I see, or hear the things I hear. I don't want to feel pain in my heart over things I can't control.

But Grandma gave me the cure. In my soap dish is a big fat bar of Safeguard. I peel off my clothes and hop into the shower. I lather up, close my eyes, and breathe deeply. I think about that little plastic turtle soap dish. And within seconds I am back in Grandma's tub, safe and sound. And I know everything is gonna be all right.

The Umbilical Cord is Never Cut

Today my Mother has gone home to live alone for the first time in her life. With the urn containing what is left of my Step-dad's physical body strapped firmly into the passenger seat next to her, Mom drove away from my little Sister's house where she has been staying since Jim passed away.

I would say I can't imagine what was going through Mom's mind as she left the busy city and headed out into the countryside to face a new life without her husband by her side. But I can imagine. She is my Mother. The umbilical cord is never cut.

Even though she is over a thousand miles away, my heart hurts today because I can feel her pain. I know, on a much smaller scale, what it feels like to lose the one you love. I know that utter sense of isolation and loneliness when you awaken at three o'clock in the morning without your beloved next to you. The whole world is asleep and you are the last living soul on the planet. It is just you and your thoughts and a deep, dark stillness.

Then morning comes and there is no escaping the fact that you are utterly and completely alone. No one there to say "Good Morning!" No one taking up the bathroom. No one to give you a kiss and a hug or pour you a cup of coffee. It is just utter emptiness. Your soul feels like a bottomless well and you are falling. You will never hit bottom nor will you ever will return to life. It is the great void, the absence of all that is love.

There are no words of comfort that can take away the pain of a loss such as this. It is something we humans all must go through if we dare to love. The only medicine is time.

Christmas Cards

Grandma kept a special address book for Christmas cards. It held the addresses of most everyone she knew for the last forty or fifty years. Some were crossed off due to death. Others had new last names.

All the cards Grandma received were placed in a table top wicker basket that was shaped like a sleigh and spray-painted gold. News from Florida. New York. Mississippi. All sitting atop her round, birch laminated coffee table alongside the milk glass candy jar and several angels. The year Grandma died I had to answer her Christmas cards.

My Christmas cards are taped around the wooden hallway door frame. In other houses I taped them to doors. At the peak of card giving, I had two doors covered with beautiful notes of joy and celebration. When I moved into my new home in 2006, that first Christmas saw two door frames covered with swinging Christmas cards. Two! Photo post cards of my friends Daria and Virginia and their two girls, another friend with her dog. Christmas letters telling of the year's adventures. Cards shaped like they should hold money or a check, but they don't. Cards shaped like they wouldn't hold money or a check but they do.

There are Jesus cards and silly cards and funny cards and nature cards. Dogs peeing on snowmen and Wise men delivering gifts to the babe in the manger. There are sparkly cards and handmade cards, cards from Target and cards from Hallmark. I love them all.

But a sad thing is happening. Every year the number of cards is declining. Not due to death or divorce or moving oversees or changing religious preference. Maybe it is the email and ecard thing. I don't know. Maybe I am losing friends. I have only half as many cards on my door frame as last year. Even the grocery stores, which used to have bins of Christmas cards, are cutting back. I couldn't find any nice cards this year. What is happening to this wonderful tradition?

The Mystery of Death

Once I had a dog named Idgie. One day a contractor left the door open at the house I was living in and Idgie bolted. For three days I searched for her, put up fliers, called all the local veterinarians, and reluctantly surveyed all the busy roads for her body. Time stopped. Everything was surreal. I tried to tune in to my psychic self to connect with her via our heart connection. But there was nothing. I was bewildered. I just could not find my footing. I needed to know where she was. I was full of anguish and panic. The not-knowing tormented me. It reminded me of what I experience when someone dies.

I think there are three great mysteries in life. Birth, Love, and Death. With Birth, I ask "Where did you come from?" In one second no one is there, and in the next a Spirit has appeared in the form of a body. Just like that. With Death, I ask "Where did you go?" I enter into a state of bewilderment and anguish. It is the time right after a person's Spirit leaves their body that I panic. "Where are you? I can't find you, please! Where have you gone?"

For some reason this creates a deep tension in me. I am a Spiritual person and I believe a recently departed soul is on his or her journey to the place of the Ancestors. But that doesn't help alleviate the sense of confusion I experience when they are gone. I remember when my grandmother passed. As funny as it sounds, there was a part of me that was confused by the fact she left all her things behind. They only had life when they were connected to her. In her absence, they were lost and lonely, no longer with purpose. They became things. Not Grandma's things.

My step-dad Jim learned to carve wood in his later years and he made some beautiful creations. I can only imagine if he would have learned as a boy, he could have been a Master. He was an incredible organic gardener before organic was mainstream, and he loved mushrooms and fishing. Every spring I would send Jim and my mother a mess of morels.

Jim was in the hospital the last spring of his life. I told him I would send a bag of morels and have my little sister cook them up and take them to the hospital so he could enjoy them. But neither spring nor Jim cooperated with my intentions. One evening around supper time, my step-dad left this world after a long struggle with cancer and other health issues. He and my mother live in Texas. Well he used to. Or maybe he still does I don't know. I have lost him. I don't know where he is, I do know I can't call him to ask a question about house paint or wood or mushrooms. In fact, I can never call again. I have lost him and I don't know where to find him. I am bewildered.

Back to the story about Idgie - after three days I received a call that someone had a little white dog curled up on their front porch, a very dirty white dog that was absolutely exhausted. I drove as fast as I could to that house and scooped her up in my arms. A sense of relief washed over me and I cried. I had found my friend.

I'll never find Jim on a front porch. But in time, the feeling of Jim being lost somewhere will pass, and I will know that he is right where he belongs. But until then, I am still searching.

My Name is Barb and I am a Whistler

"Barbara Jean, quit whistling!" my mom would yell, exasperated at my serenading her in the kitchen. That was the best place in the world to whistle, it was so LOUD! Of course, I would continue to whistle until she yelled three times, then I would acquiesce to her demands.

I am not sure when I started whistling, it seems like I have been doing it all my life. That is the thing about whistling, it just happens. You don't really pay attention to it. It is like breathing.

There is a cafe in the building where I work and the woman who runs it is blind. She recognizes me by my whistle as I walk in the door, but the first time I visited her cafe she thought I was a man. I never thought about whistling and gender before. I told her no I am not a man, and yes, I love to whistle. She smiled.

Then there was that day I walked out of the bathroom, whistling of course. Large bathrooms are even better than mom's kitchen. "Oh, so YOU'RE the whistler," said a woman on her way in. Busted. No privacy for me in the stall, I thought.

Many people have told me how much they love to hear me whistle, how it reminds them of someone long gone. I guess it is a dying art. I usually only see old men in bib overalls whistling in the Farm and Fleet Store. Maybe farmers are just happier people?

Why do we whistle anyway? Is it to attract a mate? Hasn't worked for me yet. Is it a physiological expression of happiness much like tears are of sorrow? I would agree with that. Whistling makes me happy. And when I am happy I whistle. A positive feedback loop.

Perhaps it is an evolutionary link to the days when we were once bird-like. Oh wait, we crawled out of the primordial ooze as reptiles. But birds originated as reptiles, right? Hmm. Fascinating.

I was standing in line at the grocery store one day when the person behind me started whistling. I was startled to hear a fellow whistler, and turned around only to see it was a woman whistling! I said to her, "Hey! Another whistler like me!" We talked about our love of whistling and found we were both unable to control the little tunes that pop out of our pursed lips.

The only other female whistler I ever saw was at a nursing home in Indiana. The entertainment of the day was a woman who whistled to cassette recordings of tunes from yesteryear. She would stand there holding her microphone and whistle away to the captive audience. Interesting. Never thought of doing that.

One place I worked had a very unhappy secretary whom nobody liked. Many times a day I would have to walk through the office area to get to the copy machine. Sometimes I would whistle. Well, OK, probably lots of times I would whistle. One day she yelled at me. "Will you please not whistle in this office?" she said, not very nicely. I guess whistling was too happy for her grumpy demeanor. It was carpeted for gosh sakes, not like a bathroom or a kitchen!

If you are a woman, like to whistle, and believe in superstition, don't read Wikipedia's entry on whistling. You will find out that in the Philippines it is improper for women to whistle in public. The U.S. Navy has a saying that only homosexuals whistle. In old England, the saying was "a whistling woman never marries." Oh god, why didn't anyone tell me these things when I was but a child?

Someday I hope to attend the International Whistler's Convention in South Carolina. Check out the site, there are some videos of award winning whistlers. I listened to a few of them, and I must say I think I could hold my own pretty well if I practiced up a bit. Now a word of caution, if you have never seen a whistler perform, it does look a bit strange, but you get used to it.

Well I say, if Snow White says it, it is good enough for me. Give a little whistle!

Yearning for Christmas

There is a huge part of me that loves Christmas, that is to say the ones I remember from my childhood. Christmas began with the long trip from our house in central Ohio to my Grandparents' home in northern Indiana. I knew we were getting close when we crossed the bridge over the Maumee River in Toledo. My Grandparents' cinder block house was built into the side of a hill, and the driveway wound around to the backside of the house. It was surrounded by snowy woods full of hickory and sassafras trees. The lower level, which was entered from the rear, had a finished basement, tool room, and bathroom on the north side and a two-car garage on the south side. A carpeted stairway went up the middle. In the basement was a kitchen, a beautiful field stone fireplace built by my Grandpa, and Grandma's working 1920's player piano, which gratefully now lives with me. Grandma kept Christmas lights strung around the ceiling all year long. This basement was the place of singing and card games and sitting in front of a fire. It was a magical place.

But back to the story. We would all pile out of the car, bags and packages in hand and enter our family home. There, at the top of the stairs, the wooden door would open and Grandma and Grandpa would be waiting with open arms and hugs and kisses. And just behind them, one of the most wondrous things I have ever laid eyes on. The Christmas tree. Their tree was always flocked to create the illusion of snow covered branches, which were then covered with beautiful old-fashioned glass ornaments. And tinsel. Lots of tinsel, which was made of lead! My eyes would immediately dart to that space under the tree, which was usually overflowing with packages. My sisters and I would race to the brightly wrapped boxes, scanning each and every tag for our names. There's one! There's another! Oh, the anticipation was overwhelming. What was in the boxes?

Frankenmuth has nothing on Grandma. She loved Christmas and her house transformed into another world. Santas of all sizes appeared in every room, little reindeers and elves, garland and candy dishes. Large plastic candles on the porch. Green and red placemats and runners covered tables and counter tops. Angels took over the bathroom with a herd of reindeer. Wreaths were hung on the walls and door. You couldn't help but catch the spirit of the holiday.

The night before Christmas was spent trying to sleep on the pull-out davenport in their study. The three of us girls would all sleep in that bed, with the door closed. Directly in our line of sight, if the door was open, was the Christmas tree. Can you imagine having to lie in bed for hours staring at a door that blocked your view of the most incredible sight a child could ever see!

But soon, eyes grew weary and before I knew it, morning came. It was still dark of course, but that didn't stop me. I jumped out of the bed, flung the door open and stared wide-eyed at the tree, its colored lights glinting off thin strands of tinsel. The whole tree seemed to glow! And then the realization hit me, Santa had come! I would shout to my sisters "Get up! Get up! Santa came!", and then run to my sleeping parents and grandparents, imploring them to get out of bed and come open presents. The whole thing was just magical, plain and simple.

Those memories are imprinted in my brain. That is what Christmas is to me. And the hell of it is we grow up. Life happens. Parents' divorce. Grandparents die. Family moves away. Houses are sold. But Christmas still comes. It is a constant reminder of a simpler time. A time of childhood, when magic and wonder rule. A time when many Elders were still with us, including my great-grandparents. A time before divorce. This is how my child mind remembers it.

So, is it any wonder Christmas is depressing and confusing? I am no longer a child but I still believe in Santa. I yearn to return to that magical tree and my loving grandparents, instead of waking up in an empty house devoid of the sounds of my family.

Dear Grandma

Dear Grandma,

Just wanted you to know I am thinking of you today, the seventh anniversary of your passing. Don't worry, I won't cry. At least not too much. I know how you feel about that. "Quit your crying," you would tell me. I can't help it Grandma. I miss you.

I wish you could have seen the fall colors this year. Up here in Michigan we had one of the most beautiful displays I can remember. Now, I know you hated the fall. I don't blame you. Grandpa, your Sister, and your Nephew all died during the season when the hickory trees in your yard were brilliant yellow. That must have been so very hard on you. And then what did you go and do? Die on October 24th! Well, no matter what you say, I think the fall is absolutely beautiful and it was a fitting time for you to go home.

A new friend of mine has given me lots of hickory nuts, and every night when I come home from work I sit and watch some TV and crack nuts for hours. I am watching the Mason jar starting to fill, it is almost halfway there. I remember watching you bent over, clad in your mother's red plaid wool jacket, picking up hickory nuts from your yard. You showed me how to tell the good ones from the bad. I could bet the farm that when I would come home to see you there would be dozens of hickory nuts spread out on your patio table. I loved that about you Grandma. And I made it a part of me. Thank you for that.

I know you would be proud of me working for the State of Michigan. I would love to tell you about all the things I am learning. You were always the one I shared everything with. My hopes and dreams, my heartbreaks and my joys. You were my best friend. I cherish the memory of our talks as we sat in the matching blue recliners, watching TV and critiquing all the commercials. I remember when you were so sick and I told you I didn't know what I would do without you. You told me I would be just fine. And that you weren't going to die for a long time. Within three months you were gone.

I have tried to go on with my life, Grandma. But it isn't the same without you. There is a hole in my heart that I don't think can ever be filled. Too much changed when you left. There is no home left to go to. The family no longer celebrates holidays together, something we did since the day I was born. There are no more honey-do lists. Or pot roasts made special just for me. I think that hits the nail on the head. No one has ever made me feel as special as you did. Now I feel very alone in the world and not really special to anyone.

So, I guess what I want to say to you Grandma on this special day, is thank you for the tender and sometimes tough love you gave to me, for being there when I was at my lowest, and being there when I was at my best. For sharing your stories and laughter and struggles and regrets. For teaching me to be kind and work hard, and to have strong values and a strong work ethic. Thank you, Grandma. I will always hold you close to my heart.

With love,

Your #1 Granddaughter, Barbie

Coming Home

I remember it was fall, October I believe, in 1998. I had been driving nine hours in a fourteen-foot Ryder truck which contained all of my belongings. My dog Idgie and I had traveled across the Cumberland Mountains, over the flat land of Ohio, and into the northeastern corner of Indiana. I pulled into the familiar winding driveway that took me around to the back of my Grandma and Grandpa's house. I had come home.

Grandma and Dad were waiting for me. Grandma had her hair covered with a scarf and wore her mother's red plaid wool jacket. She had on her work "sneakers" and was ready to unload. We spent the next several hours emptying out the truck into her garage. I was exhausted.

Grandpa had passed away in 1997 and Grandma was understandably still quite heartbroken. Life must have felt very empty in the absence of her other half, someone she was married to for nearly fifty years.

I had been in Pennsylvania since 1992 and most of those years were spent battling depression. By 1998 I was out of a job, broke, and heartbroken. I needed Grandma. She needed me. So, I went home.

For the next two years Grandma nursed my wounded soul back to health. I tackled her "honey do" lists, tried to get her to eat morels, and helped her learn the computer. We watched TV together, ate ice cream together, and laughed together. Sometimes we cried together.

Grandpa's chair was no longer empty. I also took over some of Grandpa's jobs. Like cutting fresh pussy willows for Grandma in the spring. I decorated the Christmas tree. I mowed the lawn. I critiqued commercials with her. We had a good life.

I got better, and Grandma began to smile again. When it was time to move on with my life and return to Michigan, I promised Grandma I would always be there for her, like she had been for me. I hugged her long and hard, and smelled her soft gray hair. A part of me didn't want to go. I wanted to stay in Grandma's love forever.

Those two years were some of the most precious of my life. Grandma became my friend, my confidant. She learned my darkest secrets and my greatest triumphs. I learned the story of her life, her childhood, her tragedies, her fears. I saw a strength in her I never knew existed. I learned her greatest regret was not joining the Armed Services. She would have been good at that. I saw a woman with a heart so big it could have encompassed the Universe. What a blessing.

The Perfect Food

Grandma Barton used to eat a sundae for dinner most nights of the week. "I believe I'll have a dish of ice cream," she would say to me from the comfort of her sky blue Lazy Boy recliner. "I'll get it. Do you want nuts?" I would ask from Grandpa's sky blue Lazy Boy recliner. "Oh yes," she would reply. "Bananas?" "Sounds good," she would say. Off I would go to the kitchen to pull out the pail of ice cream from the freezer. Vanilla with chocolate swirls. Grandma had a stack of ice cream pails in the cupboard. They were useful for many things.

I would scoop out several round balls of this delicious treat and place them in our bowls. I would then add Hershey's chocolate syrup (or whatever was on sale at the time), slice up some Dole bananas, and sprinkle with dry roasted peanuts. Jab in the spoons and we were good to go.

Back at the Lazy Boy ranch, we would settle in to eat our sundaes and watch Jag or Xena. "Grandma, you know you really should eat a healthier supper," I would lecture. "I am 85 years old. Hasn't hurt me yet," she said proudly. "I guess you're right," I said, eating another bite dripping with chocolate syrup.

My beloved and I have started a similar ritual. We both used to get those ice cream cones from the ice cream truck when we were kids, you know the ones. Ice cream in a waffle cone, with chocolate and peanuts on top, all wrapped in paper? Our local grocery store carries them, so when we need a little dessert, we stop in for a mini sundae.

These cones are the perfect food. A little dairy (ice cream), some protein (nuts), carbs (waffle cone), and dessert (chocolate). The green? My dollar I give the cashier. Grandma was right. Sundaes are good for you and healthy, too.

Grandma is gone now, but every once in a while, I still fix myself a hot fudge sundae with Dole bananas and dry roasted peanuts, put on an old episode of Jag, and sit back in Grandma's old sky blue Lazy Boy. Just for old times' sake of course.

Happy Birthday Grandma

"At night when it was time to go to bed, Dorothy and Lana would make me go up the stairs first. They held the candles, and up the stairs I would go. As soon as I was halfway up, they would blow out the candles and start stomping their feet. "Phyddie there's a bear, run Phyddie there's a bear!" I would race up those stairs lickety split, scared out of my wits."

"Well, one day I was out to the barn with my Dad and I found a dead rat. I picked that thing up by the tail and asked Dad if I might have that old rat. Sure, he said. So, I put that rat behind my back and found Dorothy. I walked up to my sister and pulled out that rat and chased her all around the barn and back again! She was a screaming and hollering, my sister, they never told me there was a bear again!"

"Another time, why I was just a young girl, my Dad told me to take the car and drive down to the creek to get us some water. I couldn't believe he would allow me to do that! So, he put the old milk container, you know, those big metal milk cans? He put that can in the back of the car and I drove off down the lane to the creek. I filled up that milk can with water at the spring and drove back home. My Mother was beside herself! Dad said I could do anything I set my mind to. I never forgot that."

On July 26, 1918, Phyliss Hope Barton was born in Steuben County, Indiana. Phyddie, as she was called, was a blond haired, blue eyed beauty who loved cooking, bowling, shows in Chicago, Patsy Cline and Nat King Cole, Yahtzee, the Moose Lodge, and traveling with her girlfriends. But most of all she loved her family. All our gatherings were held at Grandma's house in the later years. The fire was lit in the basement fireplace, the player piano started, and the whole extended family would sit around Grandma's large dining room table eating foods that Grandma spent a week cooking. Or maybe pulled out of the freezer from our last meal together a year earlier. There was one particular fruit cake that came out of the freezer every holiday for three years. She threatened that it would continue to go back in the freezer

47

until it was eaten up. She wasn't kidding. Those were great times.

Grandma Barton helped me through the darkest time in my life and gave me the love and security to reclaim a life almost lost to depression. She was my worst critic and my biggest fan. And my world hasn't been the same since she left us.

On this day, the day Phyliss Hope Barton was born, I honor her memory and feel so blessed to have had her in my life. She left some big shoes to fill.

When Do People Choose to Die?

Death is one of life's greatest mysteries, something that happens to all living things, except Vampires of course. The body ceases to function and just quits running. It turns cold. And the person or dog or cat we knew is gone forever. It stuns us. It confuses us. Where did they go? That is the mystery.

Some folks believe that we choose the time of our birth and the time of our death. I have heard many people say how so-and-so waited until the family was together before passing. I think there might be some truth to this.

My Grandma Barton did not EVER want to talk about death. She believed herself to be immortal. "I am not going to die," she would often say. But really, she was afraid. She liked to have control of things in her life, and the mystery of Death is controlled by no one.

After Grandpa passed in 1997, Grandma stayed in her house on the hill in the woods. She had a set routine. She would start the coffeepot in the morning, walk out to the mailbox to fetch the newspapers, and sat down in her recliner with her Irish Creamer-laced coffee, two oatmeal chocolate chip cookies, and the papers. On went the TV and she would watch the last half of the morning news, then her favorite shows JAG and Walker Texas Ranger. She would then do her chores, work on the books for the Moose Lodge, check her email, do some cooking, and maybe run an errand or two. Evenings were watching Xena, Star Trek, or whatever else she could find. If she were to awaken at say one o'clock in the morning, which was not unusual, Grandma would turn on the TV and watch Disney's Zorro, the old black and white version.

Grandma was eighty-seven years old in 2005. She still participated in the International Women's Bowling League and cooked every weekend for banquets and dinners at the Moose Lodge, where she also held office. Then she got breast cancer.

Grandma had already planned to go on a cruise to Alaska in June of that year, so she told her doctor no surgery until she got back. Fortunately, it was in the early stages and the surgery was very successful. She was going to be alright. But then she had a heart attack which turned into congestive heart failure, and in October Grandma met the great mystery of Death.

A couple nights ago, I was watching a re-run of JAG (it always makes me feel close to Grandma somehow). It was the show's last episode. The date was April 29, 2005. I remember vividly watching that episode with her, and how sad she was that her favorite program was ending. She did not know she had cancer yet.

Then, Zorro was put back in the Disney vault, something the giant corporation does to make you think you will never ever see that show or movie again. Then, oh, maybe a few months later, they will release the show on DVD and make a million dollars off your relief. Anyway, Zorro was a show Grandma loved, and it was now gone.

So, I got to thinking, as I was watching the end of JAG's last episode, whether the losses of these familiar faces, Mac and Harm and Zorro, might have tipped Grandma toward considering moving on, subconsciously of course. I mean, she lost Grandpa, she was alone most of the time, and these people on the TV were her friends. I understand this. I am alone almost all the time. The people on my favorite TV shows are always there. I spend more time with my TV friends than my real-life friends. They are too busy. But my TV friends, they are loyal. You get attached to them. I remember when I saw the Star Trek movie where Spock dies, I cried and cried and was devastated for days. Spock couldn't be dead, he was part of my life since I was a child! [Barbie, this is your Grandma. You need to see your doctor, honey]

So maybe the loss of those TV friends made a hole in Grandma's life, maybe times changed to the point that life became unfamiliar and wasn't going to get any better that way. She could no longer drive, she could no longer breathe, she could no longer walk without a walker, and she could not watch JAG or Zorro anymore, all in a period of three months. So maybe she chose to exit this life for the great mystery of beyond.

Wherever you are Grandma, I hope you can watch any damn show you want to. I hope you can go bowling and dance and drive and cook and eat oatmeal chocolate chip cookies. And I hope you remember you and me watching that last episode of JAG together, tears streaming down our cheeks. We both knew it was the end.

Buffalo Nickels

The laminated birch headboard on my Grandparents bed had two little cubby holes on the ends with an open space in the middle. Grandma must have really loved this type of laminate, because her dressers and living room furniture were made from it.

Whenever I went to visit Grandma and Grandpa, one of the first things I did was to enter their bedroom. On the north wall hung photographs from ceiling to floor. On the west wall you could look out the window and see the pond in the woods. To the left of the window was a latch hook rug and to the right hung photographs of several generations of our family - the most important thing in the world to my Grandma.

But my favorite thing in Grandma and Grandpa's room lived in Grandma's cubby hole. Hidden behind the gold handled door were two mason jars. Both were filled to the brim with buffalo nickels.

I would take those jars out, dump the nickels on the bed, and hold each one in my hand, marveling at the weight and detail of these old coins. My imagination would wander back to the time when buffalo roamed the prairies and plains by the thousands. As a child I had not yet learned about the slaughter of the buffalo and the Indians. I just knew those were magical coins that held special powers. Just what powers were a mystery to me, but they were magical just the same.

Not long before she died, I asked my Grandma what made her start collecting buffalo nickels. She said, "Oh, I don't know. When I was young I thought they were beautiful and just started collecting them. Before I knew it, I had two jars full! Not only did Grandma think buffalo nickels were beautiful, she loved two-dollar bills and stashed those away as well.

In 1999, the U.S. Mint started producing state quarters, each with a unique design. Then, in 2005, they started making beautiful nickels, and one design features the buffalo. It was the nickels that caught my eye.

There is a jar sitting on the counter by my backdoor. In this jar is a collection of beautiful nickels, pretty state quarters, interesting pennies, and some foreign coins I have found along the way. The only thing missing is a curious child.

Pie

I am a pie baker. Not the kind of pie baker who buys those frozen crusts from the freezer section of the grocery store, then takes them home and fills them with god knows what. I am a bona fide dyed-in-the wool, make-it-from-scratch pie baker, just like my Grandma Aldrich. The only difference between us was she used butter and I use Crisco in the crust. Other than that, I think Grandma would be proud of the creations that come from my kitchen. One of my favorite recipes is Grandma's Homemade Butterscotch Pie. Divine.

We are a rare breed nowadays. With places like the Grand Traverse Pie Company (GTPC) popping up across the Michigan landscape, women have traded in their rolling pins for GTPC gift cards. Pie baking is becoming a mystery, something our Grandma's used to do. Women fear a pie crust almost as much as a visit to their gynecologist.

I have learned over the years that there are certain things that give women mystical magical powers. Pie is one of those things. No matter what your request, you can make a pie and your wish will come true. Guaranteed. Why in the world would women want to give that up?

People cannot resist a homemade pie. They stand over it, drooling and marveling at the light flaky crust, the intricate lacing on a lattice top, and inhale the soul-penetrating aroma. They are transported to another time, another place, they are flooded with memories of old home. Their eyes close. Their arms involuntarily take their hands toward the pie, only to be slapped by the cook. "Not yet!" she will say. Eyes pop open and are fixated on the circular piece of heaven, and eating that pie becomes an obsession. They can think of nothing else. They are hooked.

Pie bakers stick together, but they do have their secrets for making the perfect crust and keep the cards close to their chests (bosoms?). Do they use Crisco or butter or lard? Do they use their hands to mix the dough or do they prefer a fork? What type of pie plate do they use most often? Do they bake in their Grandma's apron or stark naked? Vinegar or no vinegar?

It pains me to think of all the wonderful pie crust recipes that have been passed on from generation to generation, only to be lost to the frozen food section. Pie baking is becoming a lost art, something to be showcased at historical reenactments alongside the Civil War battles and the fur traders. Congress should throw money at preserving this important part of our heritage. What is more American than mom and apple pie?

I was so excited the day I discovered my Grandma Barton's pie basket I could have squealed. It looked just like a picnic basket but was square and had a removable shelf so you could stack two pies. I started collecting them and had about six or seven at one time. But I can't resist gifting a pie basket to another pie baker, especially those who have never seen one before. My stock is down now, but I dream of baking so many pies that each basket is filled to the brim with delicious pear, rhubarb custard, buttermilk, berry, peach, cherry, and butterscotch pies.

So, come on gals! Take back one of your mysterious feminine powers and learn how to bake pie before it is too late and all us original bona fide dyed in the wool make it from scratch pie bakers are dead! I'll be making the first rhubarb custard pie of the season tomorrow, stop on by.

Poison Ivy, Slippery Elm, and the Dope

I listened attentively as Grandma Aldrich told me a story about my Uncle Marvin when he was a little boy. "He had burned his hand real bad," she said, pointing to her palm. "I took him to a neighbor lady, she had special healing powers. When he came out of her house, there was no trace of a burn." She shook her head, still unable to comprehend this. "His hand was perfect, not a trace of red or anything." Grandma had a puzzled look on her face, still unsure as to how this miracle had happened.

Grandma suffered from arthritis and because I loved her, I was always looking for herbal remedies to ease her suffering. On one weekend visit I brought her a bottle of arnica tincture. "Here Gram, let me rub some of this into your hands, it will make you feel better," I said. She held out her soft, swollen hand and I let a few drops of the arnica coat her painful joints. With great care, I gently rubbed it in. "There, all better?" I asked. "Well, maybe a little," she lied. "I'll leave this with you and you can try it some more, ok?"

"Ok," she replied.

I called her a few months later and asked how the remedy was working. She told me it didn't really help her, but she gave the bottle to a friend of hers who also suffered from the debilitating disease. "She couldn't raise her arms above her head," Gram explained. "So, I gave her the bottle and she tried it, and my Lord she could raise her arms for the first time in years. She ordered a whole case!" That made me happy.

My curiosity about herbal medicine began in my mid-twenties. I went to a workshop on medicinal wild plants and was hooked. Grandma's story only furthered my interest in alternative healing practices, and I began my quest to learn everything I could about how plants in the woods can heal us.

Now one thing I have always struggled with is how to test the effectiveness of my herbal remedies. I tend to have the same recurring illnesses and thus not many opportunities to try things myself, and those around me have not been racing to the front of the line to be my guinea pig. What to do?

I was rock climbing one day and noticed a large patch of poison ivy at the base of an old oak tree. I had just been reading about using jewel weed and slippery elm bark to treat the extremely itchy poison ivy rash. But I didn't have poison ivy. Then my light bulb went off. Why not do an experiment like they do in the labs? I went over and picked a few leaves of poison ivy and gently rubbed them on top of my right forearm. "There," I thought. "Now I will get a little poison ivy rash and I can test out my treatments."

I waited one day, two days, three days, but no rash appeared. Not to be dissuaded, I went back to the poison ivy patch and this time I picked a big handful of leaves and rubbed them vigorously on my arm. The very next day I had poison ivy. I mean I had poison ivy. Those familiar blisters started to form, my skin was bright red, and itched like the dickens, to put it politely. Excited, I created a poultice of slippery elm bark by mixing the powder with a little water to form a paste. I covered my poison ivy rash with the sticky mixture, wrapped my arm in gauze, and went on with my day, confident my herbal remedy would have my rash cleared up lickety split.

That night I didn't sleep so well. My arm itched beyond belief. It hurt. It burned. I was miserable. When I awoke the next morning, my forearm was one solid poison ivy blister, red and swollen. I went to the emergency room. They gave me a shot, some pills, and treated my arm. "How did you get a case of poison ivy this bad?" the doctor asked.

"It's a long story," I replied.

Grandma and Patsy

Every Sunday, before she sat down to eat her cookies and drink her coffee, Grandma Barton would load up her phonograph with records. She would select four or five albums of whoever she felt like listening to that particular day, set them on the spindle, move the arm over on top of them, and turn the record player on. She must have had several hundred albums by such greats as the Mills Brothers, Nat King Cole, Dean Martin, and Willie Nelson. But her favorite was Patsy Cline.

Grandma loved to dance. Whenever a Patsy Cline song came on the radio and there was a willing dance partner in the house, Grandma would soon be swaying across the kitchen floor, singing along.

Once in a while I would play my guitar for Grandma. She used to ask me, "Why don't you learn to play some Patsy Cline songs?" I told her it just wasn't my style.

This is one of my greatest regrets in life.

I never asked Grandma about it, but it seemed like all her favorite songs were about heartache, and nobody could sing lively heartache songs better than Patsy. I knew Grandma had her heart broken pretty bad when she was a young woman, and maybe that was why those songs spoke to her. I chuckle when I think about how ironic it was that she used to complain that I never played any "happy" songs. Maybe she was wishing I didn't have a secret pain inside like she did.

My Grandma died at home and all of us were there with her. The local funeral home director, who had taken care of many of our family members over the years, came to take her body. They put Grandma on the gurney and as they started to move toward the door, I shouted "Wait!" I went to the CD player and put on Patsy Cline. Our family made a line from the dining room into the kitchen and we watched Grandma leave her home one last time, with Patsy singing "I'll be loving you...always." It couldn't have been more fitting.

58

At Grandma's funeral, I finally sang her a Patsy Cline song. My sisters and I created a medley of a few of her favorite tunes, which included Crazy, Release Me, Rudolph the Red-nosed Reindeer, then back into Crazy. We led friends and family in celebrating her love of music. Had my sisters not stood up there with me, I don't think I could have gotten through those songs. I still choke up every time I sing Crazy.

I have had many conversations with Grandma since then, letting her know how sorry I am I didn't learn those songs when she was still alive. Sometimes when I go visit her grave, I put on a Patsy Cline CD and let it blast out over the cemetery. I swear I can see Grandma dancing and swaying across the grass, gently singing along.

What Might Have Been

My Grandma Aldrich had arthritis since she was in her thirties and lived with chronic pain in her feet, knees, and hands all her life. Her discomfort caused her to walk with a slight limp. Through all the years I knew her, I never once heard her complain.

One weekend my parents went out of town and Grandma came to take care of us. I was only thirteen and not quite of the age to take on such responsibility, so Grandma was drafted.

I have two sisters, and back then I shared a bedroom with Dutchy (Diann). Little Kathee, the baby of the family and five years my junior, had her own room. Across the hall was my parents' room, with a long dresser from which I used to "borrow" quarters, dimes, and nickels emptied from pockets at days end.

It was on that dresser one day that I found a letter addressed to my Dad. See, Dad used to be a cop when I was very young. Heck, HE was very young, only twenty-one years old. One night after a scary high-speed chase he ended up in a shoot-out with the two suspects. He wounded one, and both were arrested and sent away to prison. This letter was from the one he shot and held promises of retaliation once he was released from prison, promises that were severe and involved my whole family. I put the letter down.

After an uneventful day we had our supper, watched some television, and went to bed. I slept in my parents' bed, Grandma in mine.

At some point during the night a noise woke me. I laid there silent and still, listening to every sound, every breath. Someone was in the house. I thought of the letter. I thought of my Grandma and my sisters innocently sleeping in their beds, unaware of the intruder lurking around our house.

I slowly got up and went to my parents' closet. Hanging in a holster was my Dad's pistol. Silently I lifted the gun from its leather holster and careful, quietly, made my way to the doorway. I peered into the darkness, checking to see if my Grandma and sisters were in their beds. They were. I knew what I had to do.

The intruder started making his way slowly down the hallway toward our bedrooms. I raised the gun and pointed it directly at the chest of the shadow walking down the hall. As I was about to pull the trigger, I noticed the limp.

I have remembered this story for forty years but it was only today that I asked my Dad the two questions I have always wanted to know but was afraid to ask.

Question: Was there a safety on the gun?

Answer: No.

Question: Was the gun loaded?

Answer: Yes.

I never told my family this story until today. And now, knowing what might have happened had one more second passed, I am chilled. One brief second was the difference between life as I have known it and a terrible family tragedy that surely would have destroyed us all.

The Collie on the Calendar

Many years ago, there was a small farm just north of a little Indiana town called Angola. And on that farm lived Grandma and Grandpa Aldrich. Grandma Aldrich was a tall, thin woman with rich brown eyes and a smile that would light up a room. And she made the very best pies in Steuben County, if not the whole state of Indiana.

Grandma and Grandpa Aldrich raised two sons and a daughter, all whom grew up and had children of their own. I was the first grandchild.

I visited Grandma and Grandpa one summer, and Grandma was busy in the kitchen baking and cooking and doing Grandma things. On the wall of her kitchen hung a large calendar, perhaps from the local insurance company or maybe the feed store. I knew it had to be a free one cause Grandma and Grandpa didn't have much money back then. On the top page of that particular month was a beautiful photo of a Collie.

Timmy and Lassie were my favorite TV stars back then, next to Sky King, the Lone Ranger, and Roy Rogers. I was sure that Collie was Lassie. Then again, every Collie was Lassie. Did I mention I can still whistle that famous theme song? I digress. Anyway, Grandma saw me looking at that calendar and she asked, "Do you like that picture?" "Oh my, yes, Grandma, that's Lassie!" I beamed.

Grandma wiped her hands on the dish towel and walked over to the calendar, pulling it off the nail that held it fast to the wall. She pulled open the drawer where she kept all those things that have no other place and took out a pair of shears. Carefully, Grandma cut that page out of the calendar.

"How'd you like a puzzle, Barbie?" Grandma asked. "A puzzle?" I asked, with great excitement, "I never had a puzzle before!" "Well, let's make you one!" she said.

Grandma went into the other room and returned with a thin sheet of cardboard. She took the lid off an old jar and dipped a small measuring cup into soft flour. She poured the flour into a ceramic bowl and then added a small amount of warm water, just enough to make a paste. Grandma gently stirred the mixture until it was silky smooth, then took out an old paint brush and first dabbed it into the paste, then brushed it on the cardboard. Once the cardboard was covered, Grandma carefully laid the picture of the Collie on top of it and gently smoothed out all the wrinkles with her careworn hands. She then set it aside to dry.

"How'd you like a snack to tide you over 'til the picture dries?" Grandma asked. "Yay!" I squealed, because I knew what that snack would be, my favorite snack in the world, Grandma's cherry pie. Grandma poured me a big glass of cold milk and cut me a delicious slice of cherry pie with little sugar crystals sprinkled on top. I was in heaven, sitting there eating my favorite pie with my Grandma by my side, watching the picture of the Collie dry.

It wasn't long before Grandma said, "I think it is ready!" She got her shears out of the drawer and began to cut the picture into many different shapes. Soon, the Collie was reduced to a pile of oddly shaped pieces scattered on the kitchen table. "Done!" Grandma proudly exclaimed. "Now what?" I asked. "Now what?" Grandma said, "you put it all back together!" So, Grandma helped me to put the puzzle back together, showing me how to figure out which pieces fit. Soon, the Collie reappeared.

I never forgot the love and care my Grandma showed me that day. She had little money but made me the best present any child could have asked for. A handmade puzzle created simply from a page in a calendar, some flour and water, cardboard, and a little imagination. Life doesn't get much better than that.

Grandma's Table

One of the most treasured members of my family was Grandma's dining room Table. Its top was a dark wood laminate and it was surrounded by wooden chairs with soft cloth cushions. Grandma took great care of that Table, polishing it every week when she dusted the rest of the furniture in her home on the hill.

After Grandpa passed away, I took over the duties of Table maintenance. Screwdriver in hand, I would get on my knees and make my away around the Table, tightening screws and making sure Grandma's Table was secure because a secure Table makes a secure family.

We never used plain table service on Grandma's dining room Table. It was a place to honor family. Grandma honored her family with china and silver. I remember gently taking the dinner plates out of the cabinet, their yellow forsythia flowers and gold rims greeting me every holiday season. We would set the Table, making sure every flower pattern was just so, the salad plates in their proper position. The silver would be polished up and placed around the beautiful china, with the forks elegantly resting on paper napkins folded into triangles. The china coffee cups and dessert plates were stacked on the counter that once held a big aquarium full of black guppies. Candles were lit and the Table was ready to receive Grandma's honored guests.

We were sitting around that Table when news came one snowy Christmas night that one of my grandparents' friends, a truck driver, missed a curve over by the motel and crashed. He didn't make it, someone said. People gripped the Table for support. Some leaned on it. The adults sat around the Table for a long time that night, seeking comfort from the Table and each other.

The Table witnessed many things in our family, including the rituals people do as they get older. As Grandma entered her eighties she began to sort. She sat at the Table, going through her old black book and pulling out all the recipes she had collected over the years, re-gluing and re-organizing them by section.

Grandma took great care to be sure that the surface of her Table did not get scratched while working on her recipe book by putting a nice white linen tablecloth down to keep it safe.

Once the recipe book project was done, it was time to sort out family photos. Grandma brought out several stacks of photo albums and set them on the Table. You could almost see the Table smile, glad to see the familiar faces Great Grandpa Zimmerman and Uncle Cully and Aunt Dorothy once again. A great sadness was beginning to settle into the Table's heart, as every year the family dinners grew smaller and smaller.

It was at this Table that my Grandmother sat weeping in my arms, somehow realizing yet not quite believing her life was coming to an end. After I put her to bed, I lay my head down on that Table and cried. In the little pool of tears, I saw a reflection, first of me, then of my Grandma.

When Grandma left us, we stacked boxes on the Table and sorted for weeks. I took home everything I could fit in my house so I could have Grandma with me every day. Her rolling pin, cast iron frying pan, the player piano, her cookie cutters. But I couldn't take the Table, I had no room. The Table along with the rest of Grandma's life things was soon gone, sent off to be sold at a tag sale.

Around that Table had sat my Grandpa and Great Grandparents, Great Aunts and Uncles, old family friends, all now gone. And when Grandma and her Table left us, our family gathered no more.

A couple years later, I wandered into an antique store in the town my Grandma had lived most of her life, the town in which I was born. As I made my way around the basement I came to a door that opened into a small, dusty, unlit room. And there, with its chairs stacked neatly beside it, was my Grandma's Table.

I took out my bandana and slowly wiped away the dust, shining it up the way Grandma would have done. And I very carefully checked every screw.

God Help the Confederates - Diann's Coming

This week my sister Diann is on a vacation. She and four other women have hopped on their motorcycles and are driving to South Carolina for sightseeing, reveling, relaxing, and bike riding. I might add here that my sister is over fifty.

Ever since learning about her trip, I have found myself worrying like a mother hen. I didn't tell her of my concerns, but I noticed my level of anxiety increasing daily up to the morning she left. What's worse is she didn't even call to say goodbye! Oh, all right, it is true her biker buddies rode in Friday night and she had a house full of company, but geez! I am her big sister and she could have called to reassure me she was well prepared and didn't forget anything like her toothbrush and hand gun... But nooooooo, she chose to hang out with them and ignore my worries.

Now, Diann has gone on vacations before, traveling to Brazil on numerous occasions, all by herself. But this time it is different. She is on a Harley. All kinds of things could happen. Why, a bug could fly in her mouth and she could choke to death! Or maybe she and her friends stop somewhere in the mountains to get a drink and take a rest. Banjo music flows out of the hills, a familiar tune. Dada da da da da da da da. A guitar answers. Oh god.

Of course, Diann researched the political climate and informed me how dangerous it will be for five liberal women on motorcycles. After all, everyone down there will know they are liberals just by looking at them. I have seen Diann on Facebook. I know how she gets when a conservative says something stupid. God help the Confederates.

Since being involved in a motorcycle accident when I was a teenager, I have only ridden on a motorcycle once. I will never ride one again. There are too many things that can go wrong, none of them under my control. And the consequences can be very bad. I know what it feels like to have asphalt cut out of my skin. I know what road rash feels like. I know what body trauma feels like. No thanks. If I need to feel the wind in my hair and the exhilaration of speed, I will take my six-year-old Jeep Liberty out on I-96 and put the pedal to the metal. I will roll down my window and stick my head out. Need filled. And I will live to tell about it

I remember Diann's driving habits when she was a teenager and they haven't changed much. She likes to go fast. Blame it on my Dad, who got us into hydroplane boat races when we were wee ones and graduated us to snowmobile racing in our teen years. Blame it on my Mom's beautiful, sleek Firebird, which ran like the wind. Or the very fast mini-bike we used to race up and down the street. The need for speed is in our blood. A dangerous thing when you are on a Harley.

I have tried calling Diann several times and her phone goes directly to voice mail. Is she in jail already, having punched a white ultra conservative Baptist with a southern drawl in some greasy diner because he made a disparaging comment about President Obama?

My hunch is Diann is having the time of her life, being with friends and motorcycles, exploring a brand-new land and learning all she can about the people there, particularly those less fortunate. That is how my sister is. She used to tell me that her family would drive to Chicago and go to the slums, so that they could see for themselves the poverty they had heard about. She did the same thing in Brazil. She has a big heart.

I think I am worried about my sister this time because we have become so close over the past few years. She is my biggest fan, always has my back, keeps me entertained, and is one of the greatest inspirations in my life. We didn't always get along, but today we are the best of friends. I hope she is laughing with her buddies, bitching about the conservatives, eating southern cooking (the best!), absorbing the beauty of the Smokey Mountains, and learning many new things so she can come home and share her stories with us.

But until then, I will keep dialing.

67

My Little Sister

I am the oldest of three girls born into our family. I have two wonderful sisters and although we all fell from the same apple tree, one bite and you know you have a Granny Smith, a Northern Spy, and a Gala. What is similar is that we all have the same core (issues that is). I suppose that is true for all siblings.

When we were young, I dutifully took on the role of big sister - bossing them around, playing practical jokes, ignoring them, doting on them, but always protecting them. It was my youngest sister Kathee that got the worst from me, although Diann would bet her first born that it was SHE who suffered the most.

Little Kathee was a happy child, always smiling with her bright brown eyes. I vividly remember her going through that stage when every sentence leaving her cute little mouth was "What's that?" "What's that?" What's THAT?" She talked all the time and seemed to have an abundance of spit, thus penny-sized bubbles would appear as she babbled on. For a while, Little Kathee was known as Bubbles.

I remember a time when Little Kathee was taking a bath. Enter big sister with a full box of Mr. Bubble. I poured the whole box in the tub and shut the sliding shower doors, just to see what would happen. Before long, blood curdling screams came racing out of the bathroom and swooshed out the front door into the neighborhood. I ran in and found the bubbles pouring over the top of the shower doors, with my little sister trapped inside a cloud of iridescent globes, crying and sputtering. Ok, not so funny.

Then there was the time she and I were down at my fort in the field behind our house. I had been practicing spear throwing and wanted to show off my new skill. "Watch this!" I said, as I threw the sharp-pointed stick carefully aimed at a spot right between her two bare feet. "Aaaahhhhhhh!!!!!" she yelled, as the spear bounced off the top of her right foot. Blood began to pour from the hole I had just created. I ran to my rustic bathroom under the pin cherry tree and grabbed a roll of toilet paper that was stuck on a broken branch. "Here, press this onto your foot and hold it there!" I instructed. I picked my sister up, she holding the bloody toilet paper roll on her bleeding foot, and me struggling to carry her up the hill to our house. By the time we got to the backyard, the neighbors had heard her yelling and came running. "Did she get bit by a snake?" someone hollered, as everyone around believed the water snakes that lived in the swamp were actually poisonous cottonmouths. "Uh, no" I replied. "I speared her." "YOU WHAAAAAAT?" my mother screamed. Little Kathee was whisked away to the local doctor for stitches. I felt really bad.

It didn't end there. Poor Kath. One of my favorite toys was my Creepy Crawlers kit. It had a square metal heating unit that held a metal mold which you filled with some unknown and probably toxic colorful substance. I would plug in the unit and watch the liquid turn into rubber worms, bugs, and troll heads. God that was cool. Little Kathee didn't think so. She was scared to death of those worms. She should have kept that to herself. One night, I put a large number of Creepy Crawlers into Little Kathee's bed. I'll let your imagination do the rest. Then, all of a sudden, we grew up.

For most of our adult lives we have lived many miles apart, she in Texas and me in Michigan. I have not been able to watch over her like I did when she was so small. Not that I should, but that is the natural instinct of a big sister. Little Kathee has faced many challenges in life since then, challenges that no one should have to go through, yet she has faced every single one with honor and dignity. No matter what life deals her, she always looks for the bright side of things, caring for others in her life, reaching out a helping hand to those in need. As many women do, she is redefining herself as she approaches the wise age of fifty, and she is an inspiration to all around her. I can't help it, but when I look into her bright brown eyes, I still see that cheerful, innocent little girl. I imagine I always will.

I am proud of my little sister and who she has become. And I attribute some of her resiliency to the early training she received from her big sister all those years ago.

Secrets

Many years ago, my mother had to have surgery to remove a growth on her esophagus so I made the trip to Texas to be with her. I hadn't seen that side of my family in nearly six years. My Grandma Aldrich had travelled from Indiana to help out and also watch my nine-year-old nephew Erik while my youngest sister Kathee was at work.

Erik had always felt a special connection to me even though we hadn't seen each other much. So, when I arrived, he was by my side every second. But the peculiar thing was he kept talking about secrets. Time and again he would bring up the subject or ask if I had any. This went on all day and it was obvious his little mind was preoccupied with the subject.

Late that night we went to bed, Erik and I sharing a room. As he tossed and turned, I could hear him sigh. It wasn't long before I asked the restless youngster what was up.

"Erik, we should get to sleep now, it is very late," I said. "Is something wrong?"

Another sigh.

"Aunt Barb, I have a secret," he said.

"Ok, do you want to tell me?" I offered.

Silence.

"Is it hard for you to say? When I have hard things to say, I just count to three and then say them," I told him.

"Ok," he said. Then I heard him whisper to himself "One, two, three…"

"Aunt Barb, I'm gay."

"Oh, that's nice," I replied. "How do you know, you are such a young fellow?"

"I have a boyfriend," he replied.

"That's nice, what is his name?" I asked.

"Moses," he answered.

My body instantly went numb. I wanted to vomit. Oh God, I had just met Moses the day before.

He was in his fifties.

Erik proceeded to tell me details of horrific sexual abuse. I tried to explain to him that Moses was an adult and he just a little boy, that if he was gay he would have a boyfriend his own age. I struggled with how to present the concept of trust, and that it wasn't his fault what happened. I promised him I would keep his secret. He finally fell asleep. I didn't.

The next morning, I sat with my Grandma and told her what Erik had shared with me. I was sick. Sick because of what happened to him. Sick that I had to share this awful, disgusting information with my Grandma. Scared that no one would do anything about it. I needed to talk to my sister first, and then call the police.

I went in the bedroom and spoke with Erik. I asked him if it would be ok to tell his Mom what happened to him. He said yes. So, I went out to the living room to make the hardest phone call I have ever made. I hadn't seen my sister in so long and this was the news I had to give her. Of course, she was absolutely devastated and broke down crying on the phone.

The rest of the trip was a blur. We kept the information from my Mother so that she could go through her surgery and heal without the stress of knowing what was happening. The police were contacted and my sister and her husband tried to get through each hour knowing Erik's life has been forever changed.

The investigation seemed to take forever. I was considered the outcry witness since I was the first person Erik had told, so the detectives contacted me every so often. During one conversation, I was asked if I wanted to hear Erik's statement. I sat in horror listening to the details of what had happened to that little boy, much of it documented in photos Moses had taken. The police found the pictures. Moses' fate was sealed.

At last, the day of the trial arrived. The sheriff's department had flown me down to Texas to testify. While we waited in the courtroom, Moses agreed to a plea deal. He was given ten years in prison. His wife, holding a newborn baby, screamed at us.

Every year, Moses would come up for parole. Every year all my family members would write letters asking that he serve his full sentence. He stayed in prison for ten years. My nephew was imprisoned in the hell of his mind for the rest of his life.

The Monster

After the trial was over and my nephew Erik's perpetrator went to jail, life went on. But things were forever changed. His stepfather could not deal with what had happened and became deeply depressed and abusive. My sister's marriage fell apart.

The abuse Erik suffered turned into a Monster inside him and began to torture his psyche. As he grew up, he became more troubled. He joined the Air Force and got married, hoping to get his troubled life turned around. But he was not looking the Monster in the eye. He hated it, he ran from it. It made him angry and violent. It made him drink and take drugs. He lost his wife and the Air Force due to the sickness taking over his mind.

There were times that my phone would ring at three o'clock in the morning. It would be Erik calling to play his guitar and show me how he was learning one of my songs. He would be drunk. I would listen, then we would talk, then there would be silence. I think he just wanted to connect.

As the years progressed, his violence became worse and sometimes turned inward. He cut himself. He overdosed. He got in horrible fights that landed him in the hospital. He broke things. He lashed out at the people who loved him. During that time, he tried to commit suicide many times.

The Monster had taken over.

I tried many times to help Erik, as I had gone through some challenges in my own life. But he never was able to join me on the healing path. The Monster wouldn't let him. In fact, he turned against me multiple times and I had to step away and watch from a distance, feeling helpless.

When he was thirty-two, Erik drank himself into a coma and nearly died. He stopped drinking for awhile after that, but still struggled with addiction. He still could not deal with what had happened to him all those years ago.

Several months after his near fatal drinking binge, Erik began to change from being violent to experiencing religion and God. He started volunteering at soup kitchens and doing other good deeds. He was also hearing voices. My sister felt he was getting better. I felt like he was still struggling, just exhibiting different behaviors from the other end of the spectrum.

At the end of his thirty-third year, Erik sent me the most loving message, words I hadn't received from him in many years. He told me he loved me and was ready to accept my help. My nephew expressed how important I was to him. How long I had yearned to hear those words. But they scared me. This was not like him.

Two weeks later he disappeared.

I will never forget the call telling me that Erik was missing. It was mid-January. Kathee and our mother, who was struggling with pretty severe health issues, were out looking for him. The police would not help as he had voluntarily left. But his mother knew something was wrong. Mothers always know.

My nephew's motorcycle was found in a nearby park, a place he loved to go to read. He was nowhere to be found.

"Is there water in that park?" I asked.

"Yes."

Something inside me filled with dread. A feeling of knowing something you would really rather not know. I pushed it away.

For two weeks my sister, my mother, and Erik's friends searched the streets and parks of the Arlington area. They sent out fliers and stood vigil at the place of his last known presence. Finally, the police began to search, too. We lived in a constant state of panic and fear. Nothing.

It is hard to describe the altered state of reality you enter when a loved one is missing. It is sheer terror. A physical sensation of numbness and nausea wash over you and doesn't leave. Your chest is tight and you can't breathe. And, of course, there are dozens of scenarios that you play over and over in your head. I swore I was going to die. I can't imagine what my sister and mother felt.

It was late afternoon when I got the call from my father. Erik's body had been found floating in the pond in the park. I broke down, my worst fear confirmed. My thoughts turned to my sister and mother, so far away. I just wanted to hold and comfort them and take that unspeakable pain away. I sobbed for hours.

Erik died from drowning though his cause of death was undetermined. If we get stuck in wondering what happened, we will only entrap ourselves in our own hell and the Monster will have new victims to torture. The Monster did not die with Erik that day. It is waiting for another victim.

We have had to learn acceptance. Acceptance that there will never be answers, that Erik is gone, and he isn't coming back. We must accept that this was the life he was given by the Creator.

Yet still, I think of that nine-year-old boy following me around asking about secrets. And the life spark that was taken by a man named Moses. Rest in sweet peace my nephew.

CHAPTER 4

NEIGHBORS

My Neighbor Kay

When I was in a rock band I had a very large and very loud Peavey amplifier. The powerful amp put out four hundred watts of sound through a cabinet containing some very large speakers, enough volume to make it suitable for playing in a stadium. So, you can imagine how my neighbor Kay felt about me practicing my electric guitar or running my stereo blasting Aerosmith through those large speakers. Kay lived across the hall from me in an old house that contained several apartments. The sounds in our apartments were hardly interrupted by the two wooden doors and stairwell that separated our living spaces.

Kay Mardis was a retired elementary school teacher, not an inch over four-foot-eight inches tall if that. She had perfectly done hair, wore thick make up on her aged face, and spent most of her days sitting in her chair chain smoking and watching soap operas. Oh, and knocking on my door telling me to turn my music down.

At this apartment house, the only patch of grass suitable for having a picnic was located directly under Kay's kitchen window. One sunny afternoon some friends and I were grilling steaks and having a good time, when Kay yelled out her window for us to keep it down. I had not formally met this grumpy old woman yet, so I marched right up to her apartment door and knocked. I was greeted by a not-so-happy Elder.

"Hi, my name is Barb and I am sorry we are disturbing you. I wondered if you might like to come out and join us for our picnic and eat some steak."

This was not what she was expecting. Her face softened and she graciously accepted my invitation. That was the beginning of our wonderful friendship.

I spent many afternoons sitting with Kay, listening to her tell stories of her life. I believe she was in her late seventies when I met her, and she had a rattling cough that came from years of smoking. It was this cough that eventually ended her life.

Kay told of a time when women were not allowed to smoke, and she and her fellow lady teachers would sneak upstairs and sit on a window ledge, puffing away and having the time of their lives. Her story was frequently interrupted by the cough, and she would have to put her red lipstick stained cigarette into the overflowing ashtray, cover her mouth and choke through another spell.

Every holiday, I would cook Kay a special dinner, usually turkey with all the trimmings. It was a ritual that I never missed. Kay had no family, she never found a special someone to spend her life with, had no children or siblings or nieces or nephews. The only folks in her life were me and two former cigarette smoking schoolteacher friends. She would open her wooden apartment door and a smile of pure joy would cover her face. I would carry the hot meal to her kitchen and she would dive in, eating very slowly and deliberating. I would also add a nice bouquet of flowers to the occasion, and I think Kay felt very special on those days. She should have, because she was one of a kind.

Over time, Kay's health began to deteriorate and she ended up in the hospital. That didn't deter my holiday dinner delivery, and all the other patients were green with envy when Kay's turkey dinner appeared one Thanksgiving Day. She ate it slowly and deliberately, smiling all the while. It made my heart glad.

Kay didn't come home from the hospital. After several weeks, she was placed in a nursing home. I stopped going to see Kay, because I found it too hard to see her in such ill health. It made me sad, uncomfortable, and scared. I didn't want to lose my friend. I didn't know what I would say to her. So, I stayed away.

I sadly remember the day when one of the cigarette smoking school teachers knocked on my door and told me that Kay had passed away. She said Kay had asked about me and wondered why I hadn't been by to see her. I felt horrible. Why had I been so selfish? I began to cry.

Her friends invited me to Kay's apartment one day and said that I could have anything I wanted, something to remember my friend by. I didn't feel like I deserved a thing. But they encouraged me, so I selected a copper bracelet, an imported salt dish made in England, a milk glass lamp, and an old trunk. I took my treasures back to my apartment across the hall and closed the door. I felt empty and sad, and diminished in some way by how I had abandoned my friend in her time of need. Kay was a dear, chain-smoking old woman who taught me many things. But the most important lesson of all was how to be a friend. A very hard lesson for a twenty-year-old young woman.

Flowers for Life and Death

I once worked in the floral business. I started as a delivery gal then graduated to the highest honor possible - floral designer. It was work I loved. Who could complain about being around beautiful smelling flowers and lush, green plants every day at work?

Life in a flower shop was like living with bipolar disorder. There were days when nobody was born or died or had a birthday or got sick. Those days were the downers. I spent hours cleaning every pebble that the potted plants were sitting on in order to prevent death by boredom. Then there was the manic phase - Mother's Day, Valentine's Day, and Christmas. Twenty-four-hour marathons of poking flowers into wet green foam called Oasis and getting dozens of bloody holes in my fingers from stripping thorns and boxing roses. Ah, I miss those good old days.

Standing behind the front counter, I was greeted with every emotion known to humans. Folks would stop in to pick out a bouquet for a friend or family member who was celebrating a birthday. They would take their time looking for just the right arrangement or container which reflected the personality of the recipient. That was especially true for the planters sent up to the hospital for the birth of a new baby or a sick loved one. There were little pink and blue ceramic lamb containers and green John Deere tractors. Tea cups and southwestern-style pots. Large handled wicker baskets that looked like a tropical forest once it was planted up. Those people always left with a smile.

My favorite arrangements to design were casket pieces. I loved the way I could let the flowers spread out like they do in nature. I was creating a living blanket, one to comfort both the dead and those left behind, the people that I found the most difficult to face. I am a very sensitive person, as you probably have already figured out. Witnessing the depth of grief in people getting flowers for their lost loved ones just broke my heart, plain and simple. Especially the Elders. Yes, casket pieces were my favorite, my way of helping comfort those families with the beauty and fragrance of flowers.

I had a boss at the last shop I worked in named Tommy. He was the kind of character you meet once in a lifetime. Tommy drove the delivery van and his wife ran the business. He had shocking white hair, black rimmed glasses, and was always on the go. Tommy had an illness that required him to take a certain medication. This drug had several side effects, one of which caused him to take frequent and urgent bathroom breaks.

Tommy and I had a ritual. Every April Fool's Day, we played a prank on each other. One year, I got to work early and snatched the child mannequin from the upstairs storage area. I strategically placed her on the toilet, as if doing her business. Now visualize the bathroom - it was long and narrow, maybe four feet across. It was a straight shot from the hall to the toilet and worked well for someone who had to get there quick.

As he did every morning, Tommy brought in a sack of fresh donuts and made a pot of Cadillac coffee. He knew I loved jelly-filled, sugar coated donuts and had several in the bag. I got my hot cup of coffee, reached in the sack and pulled out the largest one. With great anticipation I bit down and felt the raspberry filling squirt into my mouth. Along with a tablespoon full of dried onions. It was all I could do to keep from losing my cookies.

Ten minutes after drinking his first cup of coffee, Tommy ran to the bathroom ninety miles per hour. I was already cracking up when I heard him yell as he flipped on the light switch and almost sat on the poor little girl! The whole shop was laughing hysterically as we listened to him hollering at me from behind the closed door.

Tommy passed away a few years ago and I went to the service to pay my respects. There were dozens of beautiful flower arrangements circling the room along with all the stories being told about Tommy. What I remembered most was the last scene at the end of the video depicting Tommy's colorful life. He was waving from high in the sky, hang gliding behind a powerboat at the ripe old age of eighty. I hope I go out with such joy.

From the Mouths of Babes

There were two little girls that lived across the street from my house on Indiana Avenue, beautiful blonde-haired blue-eyed princesses. One wore an impressively sparkly tiara. The girls rode their bikes up and down the sidewalk day after day after day. They lived in that house since they were babes.

One afternoon the girls discovered a paper wasp nest hanging from a tree and were totally intrigued by it. Every day they would ride their bikes under it, then sharply turn around and scream, "The Queen is out the Queen is out!!!" and race back home.

One weekend I saw the two little girls, their little cousin, and a couple of high school girls approach the nest. I figured the neighbor girls were going to show the older girls their discovery.

Was I wrong.

Before I knew it all five had picked up rocks and were winding up for the pitch. I thought only boys did this kind of thing!

"Knock it off!" I yelled, just in the nick of time. I began my lecture from across the street and they sulked back to their house. It wasn't long before I heard, "The Queen is out, the Queen is out!" and saw them tearing back down the sidewalk to their homes. I had visions of wasp formations zooming out of the nest, stinging the dickens out of the girls. "It would serve them right," I thought.

I grumbled about those kids the rest of the weekend. In my mind they grew into rats, blond-haired blue-eyed rats. Stupid girls acting like stupid boys trying to kill yet another helpless little bunch of creatures.

One afternoon I went to check my bees out at a farm, then headed back home for a rest. As soon as had I pulled in my driveway, up rode the youngest girl.

"Are you the lady that yelled at us the other day?" she asked.

"Yes," I replied, waiting for her smart remarks to start flying.

"Thank you" she said. Huh?

Thank you?

Not, "You're a mean old lady and we're gonna smash your tomatoes!" She said thank you. A seven-year-old.

I told them I was afraid they would get stung. I asked if they wanted to learn about the wasps. She said she loved nature and wanted to learn all about them. So, I spent some time explaining all about the wasps, how they built their nest, how the queen hibernates in the winter, that sort of thing. Soon her older sister arrived, then they called over the little cousin. Question after question poured out of their little blonde mouths.

"If a possum or raccoon is in my backyard will they kill our dogs?" "Do you know about every kind of animal in the whole world?" "I found a bug with red legs and a red body, and it was real big. What is it?" "I found a green caterpillar and gave it leaves and it turned into a butterfly and it was so cool!" "I want to learn about moose." And on and on they chattered.

I went back into the house feeling like a jerk. Lord it's hard to be humble when you are almost perfect in every way. So, I went downstairs to my library and pulled out a selection of Golden Guides. Perhaps a gift would redeem me.

Moon of the First Spray, or, the Beagle and the Skunk

Little Skunk was stealthy. It knew the Human comes out every morning, shining a candy apple red Mag light into the darkness blanketing the backyard. Most times the light would land on Little Skunk, who was intently digging small holes in the grass, looking for her morning breakfast. Not once did she look up. Or at least that's what she wanted the Human to think. The big two-legged one did not notice that little black eyes were staring at her all the while.

One morning, Little Skunk decided it was time to make her move. It was the Moon of the First Spray. All the Skunks in her family had given a great feast in her honor the night before. And here it was, the morning of all mornings when she would make her mark and enter adulthood. Her heart fluttered. She had been practicing her shot on an old tree stump all week. She knew she was ready. Ten out of ten.

And so early that morning, Little Skunk went through the opening in the old gate and positioned herself directly behind the old apple tree, well hidden from the beam of light that swept across the yard. She waited.

"Ok little buddy, coast is clear!" said the Human. The back door opened and out came Tiny Beagle.

He caught Little Skunk's scent immediately. Tiny Beagle dropped his nose to the back steps and found the trail. Little whimpers escaped his throat as they always do when he is on scent.

"Perfect," thought Little Skunk. "He will come right to me."

And to Little Skunk he went. The second Tiny Beagle looked up and noticed the black and white furry thing in HIS yard, Little Skunk took aim and fired. It was a direct hit, right between the eyes.

Tiny Beagle began shaking his head, squeezing his beautiful

brown eyes tightly. No matter how much he shook that nasty smelling stuff wouldn't fly off! Tiny Beagle blindly made his way to the back door to be rescued by the Human with the flashlight. "Tiny no!!!" could be heard down the block, as the Beagle began to rub his face on every cloth covered object in the house.

Little Skunk stood there in disbelief. She did it! On her first try, she shot the dog right between the eyes! Cheers erupted in the dark morning forest, Skunks from all around celebrated and danced under the moonlight, their white stripes flashing brightly through the trees. A tiny acorn medal was pinned on Little Skunk by the Elder of her pack, and she was escorted to a feast of beetles and grubs. It was delicious. Afterwards, Little Skunk crawled into her burrow for a nice long nap. And dreamed of another morning, another Dog...

Fear

There was a time I was homeless, living in state campgrounds. I had to switch sites between campgrounds every two weeks. The camps were not real far apart, a few miles maybe.

One day I was driving out to one of the campgrounds when I saw smoke up ahead. As I got closer, I notice an SUV had gone off the road and hit an old willow tree, which had broken off and was laying on top of the car. Flames were leaping three feet in the air above the engine compartment and thick black smoke was pouring out of it. Inside, I could see the white-haired head of a man slumped over the steering wheel.

I immediately pulled off the side of the road and ran to the accident. For a millisecond, I went through all the possible scenarios of what could happen to me. I had never entertained the idea that I would be blown up in an explosion or burned up in a car fire. But in no way could I let a man die, so I put that deep intense fear aside and ran to the car.

The first thing I did was open the car door, and the man started to rouse. He began to fumble around for his glasses while I was trying to hold the door open with my left hand and undo his seatbelt with the right. The vehicle was at a steep angle that led away from the road, precariously situated on a slope of long wet grass that terminated in an open water marsh. After the seatbelt buckle finally opened and released, I began pulling the man out of the car.

He was a large man, maybe two hundred and seventy-five pounds or so. He landed with a thud on the ground, and seconds later the inside of the vehicle went up in flames. I let go of the door with my left hand and began my attempt to pull him up the slope and away from the car. Instead of that super-human strength that is supposed to overtake one in an emergency, I couldn't budge him. In fact, he started to slowly slide down the slope, which would have eventually placed him directly underneath the car.

85

It was in that moment a woman arrived to help me. She was a good fifteen to twenty years older than I, putting her in her late fifties to early sixties. She called 911 as soon as she came upon the accident, and then began to help me pull the man away from the flames. We made a little progress, but not much, when another motorist stopped and ran down to help us.

"One, two, three, pull!" I shouted. And we pulled. "Again!" And we pulled. The windows of the car exploded and it was totally consumed by fire at that point. I was still in great fear for our lives.

After what seemed like eternity, we got the man to the side of the road. I said we needed to keep pulling, to get away from the thick smoke filling the air, but the motorist who had stopped to help left us, saying "I am not getting sued!" And off he drove.

I tried to get the man to lay down, but he would have none of it. There was a trace of blood in his mouth, but no other visible wounds. Finally, the fire department and ambulance came and took care of the fire and the man. They told me he would surely have died if I had not come along and pulled him out of that car.

Later I learned he had two collapsed lungs, a ruptured spleen, broken collarbone, and internal bleeding. He was lucky to have survived.

I can't describe the level of fear that consumed me for that first moment. It nearly paralyzed me, but in no way could I stand by and let a man burn to death. It taught me a valuable lesson, one that I go back to time and time again. That no matter how afraid I am, I can put that fear aside and do amazing things. As Franklin D. Roosevelt once said, and I concur, "There is nothing to fear except fear itself."

The Shoe on the Road

How does this happen? You are driving down the road and there it is. A shoe. Can someone please tell me how the heck shoes end up on the road? Did someone's sister or brother throw it out the window as the family station wagon cruised down the interstate? But these aren't kid's shoes, they are almost always full sizers.

A week ago, I spotted a black high-top shoe. It was in the westbound lane of Grand River Ave, just before the railroad tracks. It looked like a nice shoe. The next day, Shoe was a few feet closer to the tracks. Fast forward to today, and Shoe has crossed the tracks and made it all the way to the stoplight nearly five hundred feet away.

Shoe is heading west.

Perhaps Shoe got fed up with its partner and struck out on its own. Perhaps it is absent-minded and simply got lost. What is really sad is that people keep running over it. No one stops to help Shoe, or ask if it needs a ride, or takes it to Goodwill. Nope, they just drive over it like they do the neighborhood squirrels, raccoons, and opossums. I bet they don't even notice it.

But I do.

I have changed my route to work so that I can follow Shoe and see where it ends up. If it gets too close to the curb the street sweeper will suck it up. Perhaps it knows this fact and that is why Shoe stays in the middle of the road. I don't know. But I look for it every morning.

Shoe must travel another fifteen hundred feet or so to reach the Grand River. By my calculations, at the current rate of travel of seventy feet per day, factoring a delay of forty-eight hours getting bounced around at each of two very busy intersections, Shoe should arrive at the River in about three weeks, give or take. Then, shoe will have to find a dog to grab it and toss it over the bridge so it can begin its big summer adventure down the Grand. Thrilling!

My only fear for Shoe is that it gets where it's going before it loses its...sole.

Update:

While driving, I was next to a car with a very active toddler in the back seat. The passenger window was open a few inches. To my amazement, I watched as he was trying to push something out the window. After much effort, the youngster finally shoved a tiny pair of shorts out into the car wind, where they swirled around before being run over by a truck. The parents were oblivious.

Now I have my answer.

The Magic Chicken

Breakfast is my favorite meal. I eat the same thing every time. Scrambled eggs, bacon, and salad. One Saturday morning, I stopped at my favorite breakfast spot. While waiting for my meal to arrive, I read a story in the newspaper about the Tour de Coop, a bicycle tour of ten urban chicken coops. How cool was that! I have always wanted chickens but didn't think my beagle and a flock of hens would play well together. Still, when I read that story, I secretly wished for a chicken.

Now you may find this very hard to believe, but I swear it is true. When I arrived home, I found a chicken in my backyard. I rubbed my eyes and looked again. Tiny, my beagle, was chasing a chicken! I grabbed the dog and put him in the house and went back outside. Sure enough, there was a Barred Rock hen, walking around like chickens do pecking at the ground. A magic chicken! The one I wished for!

I didn't know what to do! My heart was pounding. I have never known a chicken before. Well, that is not entirely true. Mr. Berry, my neighbor in Three Rivers, had two chickens that he carried around, one under each arm. Reddy and Whitey. I babysat, or "chickensat", them once. But all I did was feed them. Anyway, I figured the chicken must have flown from a coop somewhere, and it was up to me to find her humans.

I contacted a local neighborhood association, as they knew everyone in town who had chickens. I was connected to one of their staff members who had a flock. She put the word out and it spread like wildfire. "Did you lose a chicken?" was the email's subject line.

I went back and reread the article. They mentioned several chicken keepers by name, so I started calling around. I finally reached Chicken Bob. I think Chicken Bob got his name from being the first person in Lansing to have chickens. He also just got a goat and has bees on his garage roof. Anyway, Chicken Bob gave me some pointers about what to do with the chicken, who I began calling Henny Penny. He told me he would be happy to come over and build me a coop. Or, he could take the chicken and bring her into his flock. We agreed to talk later.

I went to the feed store to get some chicken feed. They were out, but said that the chicken would eat cracked corn, so I bought a bag. I was really excited to feed Henny Penny. I watched Grandma Walton do that on television so I was pretty confident. And I knew the chicken must be hungry, as the neighbors said Henny Penny had been seen strutting in the streets since at least yesterday. So, I stuck my hand in the bag, grabbed a handful of corn, and tossed it around the ground. Henny Penny came strutting over and started eating! What joy! After feasting on the corn, she went over to the dog bowl I had filled with water and she began to drink. OK. Alright. I can do this chicken thing.

Chicken Bob and I talked later. I told him no one had called yet claiming Henny Penny. Several neighbors, with drool running down their chins, said they would be glad to take the chicken. He again offered to build me a coop. Chicken Bob said I needed to make a perch for Henny Penny, as she needed to be up off the ground at night to feel safe. We agreed to talk the next day and make a decision as to whether he would take Henny Penny or we would build a coup.

I went out to the garage and looked for a suitable perch. There, resting in a corner, was my favorite hiking stick. Perfect. I mounted the hiking stick between two pine patio chairs and secured it with zip strips. Would Henny Penny find it suitable?

The rain was falling, so I knew the chicken would be seeking shelter behind the garage where I have my grill and patio furniture, protected by a metal awning. I waited an hour then snuck out. I peeked around the corner of the garage, and the magic chicken was sound asleep, perched on the hiking stick!

I could barely sleep that night, knowing that Henny Penny might lay an egg and I would get to search the yard to find it! But I was startled out of my slumber to the loud farm-like sound of "Cocka-doodle-do!" emitting from my backyard.

"NO!" I screamed!

Henny Penny was not a hen. He was a rooster.

I was dismayed. I was distraught. No roosters are allowed in the city. The chicken formerly known as Henny Penny, now Henry, had to go. My heart broke into a million pieces, for I have fallen head over heels in love with that bird. Such is the magic of chickens.

It took several calls before I was able to find someone who wanted a rooster. My friend came over later that evening after Henry had perched in the holly bush, and gently lifted him from amongst the sharp pointed leaves. Tears welled in my eyes. "Can I pet him?" I asked. "Sure," she responded. I gently stroked his beautiful feathers, steeling myself for his imminent departure. She put Henry in a box, assured me that he would be very happy living in the country with his own flock of hens, and drove him away in her pick-up truck. I waved goodbye and watched as the shortest love affair of my life disappeared in the sunset.

Oh, Henry.

The Forgotten Ones

Soon after moving in to my house, I noticed that I had a neighbor (who I will call John) that seemed quite different. Several months later, John's brother-in-law stopped over for a visit. He wanted to let me know about why I might notice that John acts different from most other folks. He told me that when John was a teenager, he was riding on the back of a friend's motorcycle across a railroad trestle over a river when the worst thing that could happen did. A train came. His friend drove the bike off the bridge and landed in the river. John landed on the buttress of the bridge, breaking almost every bone in his body. He suffered a severe head injury and his life was forever changed. His brother-in-law told me John acted "different" but was not harmful so I didn't need to be afraid of him.

It has been six years now that I have had a neighborly relationship with John. He stops by and asks if I have coffee, or a few dollars for cigarettes, or to borrow a ladder. Sometimes he completely ignores me when I say hi to him from my side of the fence. Other times he will talk my ear off, going over and over the same questions, same answers. I have found him to be highly intelligent about many things.

John is also a gifted musician and will sometimes set up his electric guitar and amp, or his drum kit, in the backyard and give a concert to an imaginary audience. Many nights I have heard him jamming away in his basement, playing along with CDs of bands from the 80's. He has told me more than once that he wishes he could play music with other people. I wish he could, too.

John has no friends. His family never visits him, with the exception of his brother from up north who might stop by once a year, but never stays. Other than that, he is alone twenty-four hours a day, seven days a week, save the company of his two stray cats. Kitty and Cat, both white, showed up as two little kittens one summer day. He tells me how lonely he is.

John has dreams. He wants to travel around the country camping, seeing all the beautiful spots. His illness won't let him. It is hard to hear the longing in his voice.

I take John food sometimes or buy him a big red jar of Maxwell House coffee. In the summer, I might take him fresh produce from the market. I give him honey from my hives, grapes from my vines, and apples from my trees. I watch out for him. And I keep my distance.

Sometimes John gets mad. Especially when he cleans his shed. He yells and hollers and swears, shouting the bad words over and over. He throws things. He talks to imaginary people. I watch.

One day a couple months ago, John came over to borrow money for cigarettes. He seemed in a good mood. I loaned him the money, which he always pays back when he gets his disability check, and off he went to the One Stop, a local convenience store. But not long after he left I heard yelling. I peered out my front window to find John standing on the sidewalk in front of my house, cursing and making threatening gestures at the neighbors across the street (who were not there). He had a knife, which he was drawing across his throat as if threatening someone with death. He shouted and stabbed at things around him. There was no one there. No one.

I called the police because I was concerned about John. I had never seen this behavior before.

A neighbor told me that John is dangerous. John had held his own sister hostage in her own house for hours, screaming at her and threatening her with his fists. That is why his family never visits, the neighbor said. I became nervous.

Yesterday, I walked in my backyard and found John sitting across the fence in his yard in the hot sun, talking to himself. I said hi and asked how he was doing. He said not so well, then started ranting about things I didn't understand. He used swear words in between non-swear words and the more he talked, the angrier he became. Something about the world and computers, and people asking if he took his meds and what business of theirs was it. He was waving a piece of paper around, which may or may not have

been the source of his agitation. He looked at me and asked, "What schizophrenic medicines do you take?"
"What?" I said.

"What schizophrenic medicines do you take?" he repeated, more agitated.

"I don't take any", I answered.

"You don't take any?"

"No."

"I don't want to talk to you get the hell out of here!" he yelled. And he shouted and he shouted. He told me to leave and called me several very derogatory names. He yelled and swore at me and started coming toward me in an aggressive fashion. I slowly walked back into my house, looking over my shoulder.

I felt afraid. I could hear him still cursing me for the next half hour as he sat in his yard or worked on his boat. I felt uneasy. He had never verbally attacked me before. I was his only friend, but that did not make me immune to his illness.

I didn't sleep well that night. I listened for sounds.

I know John is ill, but those abusive words still stung. I am even sadder, because this poor man, through no fault of his own, must live out his life literally alone. No one helps him. Society just ignores his existence, we give him some money every month but we don't give him help. No one checks on him, or visits him, or gives him counseling. Maybe someone did once upon a time, but perhaps his illness forced them away. There is no doubt that the extreme social isolation he experiences would drive anyone mad.

I feel afraid of John now. I don't know what he is capable of, or incapable of. It goes against my very nature to stop trying to be a good neighbor to him. But perhaps being a good neighbor means not giving him the opportunity to do something that could take away his freedom, for that seems to be all the poor man has.

A Jar of Honey and a Cup of Coffee

It's amazing how many of my neighbors (and I) feel isolated and alone, even though we have each other to be neighborly with. One of these neighbors is an elder I will call Mrs. Heints. I have always intended to take her a pie, but for some reason never have.

One summer, my honeybee friends graciously shared twelve pints of beautiful honey with me. I remembered that at one of Mrs. Heints' yard sales, she mentioned to me that her Dad kept bees and she had fond memories of him in his bee suit, puffing plumes of smoke around the hives. So naturally, the first person I thought of to share my honey with was Mrs. Heints. So, I scoped out her house one afternoon, saw her front door was open, and decided to visit. I went home and pulled out a nice jar of honey from the Mason jar box and walked on over to her house.

I pressed the doorbell and her little dog came barking up to greet me. Mrs. Heints had a big smile on her face when she saw the jar of liquid gold I was holding. "I brought you some honey from my bees, the first of the year," I told her. "How wonderful!" she exclaimed. "Say, do you drink coffee? Would you like to come in and have a cup with me?" "I would love it," I said, and followed her into a tiny, quaint kitchen. Mrs. Heints filled her Mr. Coffee carafe with water and poured it into the reservoir. She then took a red plastic container of Folgers Coffee from the cupboard, scooped out just the right amount, and placed the dark grounds into the basket. A flip of the switch and the coffee started brewing.

"How long have you lived in your house?" she asked me.

"I bought the house in December of 2005, and moved in early January of 2006," I said.

"Well I guess it is about time we had coffee then," she replied. "Yes, it is time," I said.

Once the pot was half full of the dark brew, Mrs. Heints took a couple of coffee cups out of the white cupboard and filled them to the brim. She sat down with a carton of half and half and for the next hour we shared stories of the Great Depression, my Grandma's life and death, her husband's death, the economy, and pondered why our neighbors don't know each other.

"That Korean couple across the street, I've talked to the man but I have never spoken to his wife. She must be shy or something, I have never seen her outside. I think it is a cultural thing," she said.

"I have a friend who is half Korean and she likes to be outside," I offered.

"Well then maybe it is just them," she said, sipping her third cup of coffee. "Hey, let me show you this," and she got up and pulled a maple leaf-shaped glass bottle down from a shelf. "It is maple syrup, a friend gave it to me."

A thin layer of mold floated on top of the syrup, barely noticeable in the narrow neck. "Nice," I said. And I thought of the shredded cheese Grandma put on my salad one day, covered in several shades of green. The eyes are one of the first things to go, you know. Not wanting to embarrass her, I remained silent.

I said my goodbyes and walked back over to my house, feeling happy. I had an Elder in my life once again. I could travel back in time through her stories, I could take her cookies and give her a hand once in a while. I could listen to her wisdom, gleaned from living eighty-five years in this world. I could learn all about the neighborhood, who died when and how, who divorced who and when, what happened to so and so, and on and on.

All because of a jar of honey. Isn't life grand?

Three Sheets to the Wind

One summer my dryer broke down. Not having any money to fix it, I strung some rope between my apple trees, bought a pack of spring-loaded wooden clothes pins, and hung the wet pile of garments out to dry. From the first towel to the last sock, I was in domestic bliss.

Women have been hanging clothes to dry ever since time began. It is a tradition that is making a comeback as folks are becoming more energy conscious. Did you know there are laws in many areas restricting clothes hanging, with some uppity folks claiming they are unsightly! Holy Moly, Mama Walton would have a hissy fit if she heard that one! Not to fear, there is a group to advocate for clotheslines. Project Laundry List is working hard to ensure everyone has the opportunity to hang their clothes on the line, and they promote air drying and cold washing as ways to save energy. Rest easy, Olivia. All is well.

What is it about hanging clothes out on a line that feels so good? It touches some primitive instinct, similar to the first time I used a blow gun. I want to pound my chest, go hunting, and scour my dirty clothes with rocks. I want to put on a paisley dress, tie a pink bandanna in my hair and swing around dancing whilst clipping my undies to the line. I want to sing songs I don't know, whistle loudly, and have a picnic. It just sends me.

"Look Daddy, there's Mommy!" I shouted when I was a five-year-old to my father as we circled above our house in a small airplane. Mom was down there hanging clothes on the line. I waved feverishly, but I knew she didn't see me. Still, what a thrill. This was my first clothesline memory.

The next clothesline memory involved not the clothesline, but the pins. The old wooden clothespins were perfect for making figures for shadowboxes. I vividly remember a Christmas scene with Santa Claus and his elves, all made from cotton balls, red and green construction paper, glitter, and of course, the clothespins. I loved those old things, so simple yet handy for so many uses.

The next clothesline memory was not so fond. The neighborhood kids and I were playing Ditch-Em at night, this was a kind of team hide-and-seek game. I was running as fast as I could to get away from an opposing player when I ran smack into that rope and raked across my eye. I couldn't see out of the swollen eyelid for days.

Today was a holiday, the first hang of spring. I tied up the thin white rope between my Macintosh and Red Delicious apple trees, got out the bag of clothespins and hung it from a branch. I ran to the basement, took the freshly laundered mint-green sheets out of the washer and proudly carried them to the backyard. I was the first in the neighborhood to hang clothes this year. I carefully folded the sheets over the line to keep them from touching the ground. The sunlight hit those sheets and made them glow. As soon as the fitted sheet was up, it billowed like a sail, blowing back and forth in the breeze. The flat sheet cracked in the wind, crisp and proper. It was as though the sheets had been set free after years of captivity, fabric butterflies wildly dancing in the cool spring air.

Clothes that are hung on the line seem to soak up every beautiful scent in the air, from the flowers to the fresh mowed grass, to the rays of the sun. The scent weaves its way into every thread and never leaves.

Tonight, I will tuck myself into bed wrapped in a beautiful spring day, with the scent of honey and sunshine and Viburnum lulling me to sleep.

So next time you do your laundry, wander out in your backyard, tie up a line, grab some pins, and enter domestic bliss. Imbue your clothes, towels, sheets, and undies with liquid sunshine. It's the closest thing to heaven I know.

Chapter 5

EARTH

Take a Walk on the Wild Side

It was an early fall day when most plants were just skeletons of their former selves, dry and snapping in the wind. I was just six years old, excitedly exploring the land behind the old Army barracks in which we lived. The Tri-Stan Housing Project consisted of barracks donated in 1946 by the federal government and turned into housing for Tri-State University students, where my father was a freshman in engineering. No longer standing, they have been replaced by Angola's Commons Park.

I made my way along the tree line and into a tangled mess of vines. There on the ground was a round, red ball. A tomato! What was a tomato doing on the ground, attached to this dried up vine? I picked it up and cradled it in my small hands. A tomato! I began to notice the plants in this spot were different than the others I had been walking through. There was more dirt and things grew in straight lines. I soon spotted another dried-up vine, and there was a cucumber! What was a cucumber doing growing on a dried-up vine? I picked the cucumber and held it in my hand along with the tomato. I was confused and delighted, all

99

at the same time.

Laying in the dirt under a pile of sticks and old plants was a board. I set my tomato and cucumber aside and pulled the old piece of wood out of its resting spot. A perfect table. I brushed off the top of the board and placed it in the sunshine. I set my tomato and my cucumber on top of the old gray plank. What else grew in this magical place?

I began searching everything that poked out of the dirt for something edible. If I didn't see anything above the dirt, I pulled the plant up to see what was under the ground. Imagine my surprise when bright orange roots greeted me! What were carrots doing buried in the ground? I placed my carrots next to the tomato and the cucumber. A feast!

That was the day I learned that food grew outdoors. I felt like I was a pilgrim, a pioneer. I was having a real Thanksgiving, just me and my tomato, cucumber, and carrots. What magic to discover my very own secret food place! Thus began my lifelong quest for wild foods.

Grandma and Grandpa's house was in the middle of the woods, surrounded by big beautiful hickory and sassafras trees. Grandma loved to pick up hickory nuts and taught me to avoid the ones with holes in them. We used the metal nutcracker and the picks to get the nutmeats out. Yummy! Hickory nuts are so tasty!

They had morel mushrooms, too. I found some giant ones in their woods one year, the kind that are a foot tall. Grandpa also used to gather puffballs and would proudly line them up on the stone wall next to their driveway. They looked like ivory basketballs.

As I got older and could read better, I checked books out of the library on wild foods. I read "My Side of the Mountain" and dreamed of running away to the mountains to live off the land. I had to settle for creating a camp in the field behind my house. I spent hours there, studying wild foods, making wild carrot stew for the neighbors, living life like it should be lived.

100

Grandma used to tell me stories of the time when she was a little girl. She said that every week a woman would come by their house pulling a big cart piled high with dandelion greens. Grandma loved dandelion greens and rejoiced when I would bring her fresh bunches of the highly nutritious leaves.

In the springtime, I head out to gather stinging nettles, dryad's saddle mushrooms, dandelion greens (for Grandma of course), garlic mustard for pesto, watercress, violet flowers and leaves, and much more. I love going out and exploring the woods and fields, seeking out foods that you can get nowhere else. There are so many nutrients and healing properties in these foods that they are well worth the time it takes to find them.

But what I enjoy more than anything else is sharing my knowledge with others. What a joy to watch someone find their first morel or dryad's saddle! Or to see their faces light up after eating the first bite of elderberry jelly on warm homemade bread. All because of a cucumber, a tomato, some carrots and a pinch of curiosity.

When Dinosaurs Stole My Heart

I tilted my head back as far as I could. There, towering above me, was the terrifying skull of Tyrannosaurus Rex. A five-foot tall Styrofoam skeleton of the most feared dinosaur ever to walk the Earth, standing there in front of me. It was Christmas and I was the luckiest kid alive.

I quickly disassembled the towering predator and took him to the basement where my laboratory was housed. Finding just the right spot, I began to reassemble the giant beast, bone by bone. The Styrofoam squeaked as I pushed each piece into its proper place. A love affair was born.

Dinosaurs find their way into every child's imagination at some point in their young lives. For children in my generation, the giants were alive and dominating the Earth at every Sinclair gas station in the 1960s. Sinclair Oil Company was founded in 1916 by Harry F. Sinclair. They began using "Dino" in their marketing and trademarked the now famous green Brontosaurus in 1932. I attribute my career as a scientist to this brilliant campaign. Did they ever imagine shaping the lives of children in this way?

A few years ago, I was driving in the countryside of Jackson County and came upon a rebuilt Sinclair gas station, complete with Dino in the yard. Not only that, they had a Petticoat Junction wooden water tower in their back yard! These were my kind of folks. Seeing the familiar symbols of my childhood brought back fond memories of my fascination with dinosaurs.

I read as many books about these giant reptiles as I could. My favorite was the one I got for free at the Sinclair gas station, called "The Exciting World of Dinosaurs". Pages and pages of beautiful color illustrations showing the large reptiles in their natural settings. I would go to sleep at night and dream of the Triceratops battling it out with my T. rex skeleton.

It blows my mind now when I think about the thirty-five-page report I meticulously researched and wrote about my favorite animals. I would sit at my little desk, with the giant T. rex skeleton looking down at me, and carefully move my No. 2 pencil within the wide lines of the notebook paper. It is true, I copied and plagiarized from the many dinosaur books I had stacked up on my desk. But hey, I was only a kindergartener. I didn't know about such things back then.

Soon I discovered models, those plastic forms that were loosely attached to a thin plastic frame. You would twist each part to break it free, then line up all the pieces in a row. Each piece had little plastic pegs or small holes that the pegs would fit into. Put a dab of that wonderful smelling glue on a peg and press the pieces together for thirty seconds. Soon, the model would become a Diplodocus or a Stegosaurus and take its place beside the giant T. rex. My basement laboratory was better than the Smithsonian.

Over time, my love affair with dinosaurs waned and I turned my attention to other things. But they still hold a special place in my heart. Isn't it something that these wonderful creatures who went extinct nearly sixty-six million years ago defined the course of my professional life? Here I am, over fifty years later, an endangered species biologist working to save other wonderful creatures from extinction. Fascinating.

The Most Beautiful Pages in the World

Collier's Encyclopedia was sold door-to-door in the U.S. from 1902-1998. I wasn't home when the salesperson came to our house at 168 Cherokee Drive in Westerville, Ohio. The books just magically appeared one day. Lined up on the shelf, they seemed to go on and on and on. I pulled Volume I from its resting place. A to Aland. I cracked open the pages for the very first time and inhaled. Oh god, the wonderful smell of an encyclopedia. Intoxicating.

I read the entire set, from Volume I to Volume XXIV. I learned about aardvarks and mollusks, Rome and Manila. Cephalopods and Cro-Magnon man, gorillas and spores. It was as if someone had put the entire world between the covers of those beautiful red books.

But my favorite of all time was Volume X, because in between Fiscus and Germanicus was Flower. Plate after plate of the most colorful, beautiful, magical flowers I had ever seen. Dutchman's breeches, those little upside-down trousers that dangle from a tiny green stem. Squirrel corn with its dainty foliage. The three-petaled trillium, which turns pink as it ages. On and on they went. I had never seen wildflowers so vividly before

I opened Volume X daily to touch the rich deep blues, greens, and yellows. Could such things really exist in the world? Well, if Collier's said they did, they did. Collier's knew everything after all, they had the whole wide world on those pages.

So, you can imagine my delight when one warm spring morning, the very day after I discovered the wildflower pictures, my fifth-grade teacher said we were going for a walk in the woods next to the school. We put on our little windbreakers and rubber boots and walked single file into the forest. We left the brightness of the sun and entered the shade of a spring canopy, and lo and behold, there before me, were the flowers from the color plates! Dutchman's breeches danced in the wind. Trillium nodded hello. There were violets and ferns, lilies and sorrels. I was standing smack in the middle of Plate IV.

It is funny how the smell of ink and the brilliant colors from a page of wildflowers can stay with you for decades. I can still close my eyes and feel that heavy book in my hands and the fluttering of my heart that spring day when I entered the forest and saw the blanket of wildflowers nodding before me. Even now, whenever I see a wildflower, I whisper thanks to my young parents for giving their hard-earned money to a door-to-door salesperson one 1968 day.

Gifts

I just finished eating a bowl of venison stew made with mushroom soup, juniper berries, dryad's saddle mushrooms, wild rice from the western Upper Peninsula, and kale from my garden. As I sat in my backyard enjoying my supper, I watched as a pair of Cooper's hawks born just this year glided between the large white oak trees that watch over my home. As my eyes traveled down the beautiful gray trunks of these wise trees, I noticed a knot hole, just the right size for a hive of bees. It was too far away for these blue eyes to see; it would take a pair of binoculars to confirm. My eyes continued on their journey, marveling at the gifts that surrounded me.

Next, they took in the grape vines that wind and twist down my old metal fence, loaded with the promise of deep purple juice in the fall. I see the dark brown seeds of curly dock which I will harvest to make a gruel. Yellow rose hips hang like ornaments on a Solstice tree, dangling from the fragrant pink rose bushes that an old woman planted long ago. They will give me a nutritious tea in the wintertime to help me keep colds at bay.

I gaze at the two apple trees that shade my bees. The Macintosh is absolutely covered in apples this year, many without a spot on them. I never use chemicals. I look over at the bees going in and out of their hives, bringing in pollen and nectar, making the most delicious honey that ever was. The pollen baskets on their legs are so big and yellow I can see them from quite a distance away. When the sun is just right, I can watch their flight paths...some flying up and out, others spiraling to gain height then disappearing over the apple trees. I wonder where they go.

My black raspberries have done their work and gifted me with many sweet juicy berries. Behind the raspberries the beautiful green leaves and tall stalks of Jerusalem artichokes command attention, towering amongst the orange-flowered trumpet vines and lavender Rose of Sharon bushes. Soon the chokes' dazzling yellow flowers will appear. But the best part lies just beneath the surface of the ground. Their tasty tubers, my favorite of all time, are to die for.

And it doesn't stop there. I look to the garden beds, so neglected by this forager, and they are bursting with color. Blazing star looks like a blue torch lighting the day. Splashes of white, yellow and orange dot the vines and herbs and climbers. New green tomatoes, starting to show color, tempt me with the promise of their heavenly taste. Cherokee purples, Garden Peach and other heirlooms I have never tried. It is not the best year for tomatoes, but still they provide.

As I sit here in my living room sharing my sacred world with you, the house wren babies that were born in the clay flower pot on my front porch are noisily begging for more food. They will fledge soon and once again there will be stillness outside my front door. I will miss them.

All these things so freely given to me by the trees and the plants and the bees and the birds. Some call them resources. I call them gifts. How blessed are we?

Snow

One winter morning when I was twelve or so, I put on my black snowmobile suit with the yellow stripes and trudged through the deep snow in the field behind my house to my fort. Falling from the sky were snowflakes the size of golf balls so I found a nice spot and stretched out in the snow. I looked up in amazement as I watched the giant snowflakes fall thousands of feet from the gray winter sky. They kept coming and coming and coming. I imagined them looking down at me, the big black blob with yellow stripes in the snow. Slowly, rhythmically they fell. A soft landing on my eyelash. A moist landing on my tongue. A crash landing on my patch that warned about yellow snow. It was one magical.

Snow is powerful. It can stop everything. It can force us to stay home with our loved ones. It can close schools. It keeps most of the bad guys off the streets and helps me feel safe at night. It records the stories of the animals as they play out their life and death struggles under the stars. It can sparkle brighter than a diamond. It can light the entire night with just a sliver of moonlight to reflect off its drifts and ridges. It can hold shadows. It gives the mice tunnels and the fox challenges. It allows us the joy of sledding and skiing and snowshoeing. And the pain of shoveling. It is one of the most mysterious, magical gifts of Mother Earth. And for that I give thanks.

Wearing a Veil

I don't know how not to care...
to pass by an animal dead on the road and not think about its
Birth and life
and tragic death.

It lays there alone melting into pavement instead of Earth.

I don't know how not to care
about melting ice caps
and drowning white bears and great Inuit Hunters
and not think about their
Births and lives
and tragic deaths.

They sink into the darkness of water which should be ice.

Alone.

I don't know how not to care
about the dying water or
watching bird and turtle and child swimming through gas and oil
unknowing of the cancer, mutation, sickness it gives
and not think about their innocence

and our guilt.

I don't know how to wear a veil that shields my eyes
from the suffering of our of world
the way some do...
those who drive over carcasses, drill for more oil
and pour poison into river without a
thought

much less a
tear.

A Divine Moment

It is hot today, so hot there are warnings. I am sitting in my air-conditioned house, looking out at the steamy air.

My shirt is damp from the cool drops of the sprinkler. You see, I was driving down my street just now and saw a large garter Snake writhing on the hot asphalt. It was trying to cross the road but was getting burned from the extreme temperatures taken in from Sun and held in the black asphalt. I slammed on my brakes and ran to Snake and tried to scoot it off the road. It had given up. It no longer tried to crawl.

I am afraid to pick up Snakes. Luckily, I had a towel in the vehicle that day. I grabbed it off the passenger seat and gently cradled Snake, who had only enough strength to spray its nasty smell as one final gesture of defense. I smiled. She was still alive. I put Snake into my car and traveled the last one hundred feet or so to my house.

What to do? I closed my eyes and listened. Coolness. Shade. Safety.

I took Snake to my raised garden beds and carefully laid her in the tall grass which grew along the wooden sides of the bed and needed trimming. At this time of day, shade now blankets the beds. Snake didn't move. I could not see her breathing.

"Come on Snake, stay with me, you'll be ok, I promise".

I turned on the sprinkler, which rained droplets of cool refreshing water onto Snake's skin. I left her there, went in the house, and prayed.

I remembered that last year, I had befriended a garter Snake I called Elizabeth. I saw her regularly, she was the most beautiful Snake I had ever seen. One day last summer, during another heat wave, I found Elizabeth coiled up by my front sidewalk, mouth agape. She had died from the heat. I took a breath and held it. Please, Creator, let Snake live.

110

After about a half hour I went to check on my new friend. She had not moved, but I did see her breathing. I again left her alone.

I waited again for a quarter hour before going out into the steamy summer evening to check on the wellbeing of my patient. She was gone, but not far. Snake was slowly making her way to my herb bed. I softly spoke to her, telling her to stay here in the yard or go to the woods behind the house. That she would be safe there. "But," I warned, "do not go across the black river. Never go across the black river." On she crawled. I moved the sprinkler so it would soak the herb bed. Snake disappeared into the leaves.

Aurora Borealis

Highway I-69 takes me from my home in central Michigan to the place I was born, Angola, Indiana. My Dad helped build part of that highway when he was a young man and I was about three feet tall. He is now retired and I am now dreaming of retiring.

Back in the early 1990's, I was traveling north on I-69 after a wonderful visit with my Grandparents. It was dark and the sky was peppered with stars. Off in the west I could see the beam of a spotlight, the kind that a business might use to attract customers, shining straight up into the night. I kept driving. Then I started thinking.

Off to the west there was nothing. No towns, no cities. No stores that would shine a spotlight up into the sky. I kept my eyes on that light, curious.

The Creator blessed me that night, for it was precisely in a random moment that I was watching the light when an arc formed around it and out poured the deepest crimson I have ever seen, as if someone had a giant pitcher of liquid color and was emptying it across the sky. Soon greens and blues appeared, swirling across the deep black sky. I blinked hard, rubbed my eyes, for a moment unable to comprehend what I was seeing. Then it hit me.

It was the Aurora Borealis, the Northern Lights.

I pulled to the side of the road and shut off my truck. As I watched the colors dancing across the heavens, I started to cry. I had never seen anything so beautiful and it literally took my breath away, moving me to tears at its magnificence.

Grandma! I had to call Grandma!

I started up my truck and raced to the rest area, which was only a few miles up the road. Thank heavens I had lots of quarters for the payphone. I began dialing. Grandma answered. "Grandma,

Grandma, the Northern Lights are out! Go outside quick and look up between your trees. I know you can see them! Hurry!" I exclaimed, barely able to contain myself. I then put in quarter after quarter, calling every person I knew to tell them to go out and look up into the sky.

Everyone at the rest area was standing outside, silent, watching the beautiful reds and greens and whites and blues swirling and pirouetting across the Midwestern sky. It was Sacred. There was reverence.

What a glorious place we live in, what amazing and awesome gifts we are given in the form of beauty on this Earth. It is beauty that must be shared when we experience it. An instinctual response put there to keep us all connected to such things that steal our breath. I hope you see something beautiful today, something that steals your breath and makes you run to the phone to call everyone you know. And I hope they all answer.

The Wren and the Bumblebee

One of my favorite memories of Grandma's home is the song of the house wren. She always had a nest box tacked to the wooden clothesline pole, and each spring the house wrens would return, singing their delightful songs.

The first year I moved into my home a pair of wrens nested in the clay pot bird house I had made. I watched their comings and goings from my kitchen window, as I had hung the pot directly in front of it. It was wonderfully healing, helping me feel close to my Grandma who had passed the year before.

I haven't seen any wrens at my house since then. Last year a chickadee family claimed the clay pot home and successfully fledged their young. I left the pot hanging over the winter without removing the old nest, thinking I would get around to it in the spring.

But then one day I heard a wren. My heart was filled with joy! I ran out back where the pot was now hanging and quickly took it down so as to clean out the old nest. I disassembled the pot and took off the bottom tray, only to find a large Bumblebee buzzing out of the nest! I placed the nest on the ground as the disoriented Bumblebee flew around. My mind only on the wren, I took the bird house to the hose and cleaned it out spic and span. I quickly reassembled the clay pieces and hung it on the front porch. I waited.

The Bumblebee didn't leave. I watched as it flew around the back door, obviously searching for its home. She didn't give up. Finally, the Bumblebee flew closer to the ground and found her nest. She disappeared under the fluffy ball. Uh oh!

I went to the front porch where I had hung the clay pot bird house, which was now to be designated a Bumblebee house. I took it down and walked back to the Bumblebee nest. Was she still there? She was not at all happy with what I had done, in fact she had me trapped in the garage for a good ten minutes. My nose pressed to the glass, watching as she tried to get in to the garage through the clear window pane, obviously wanting to give me a taste of her mighty stinger. I couldn't blame her.

I cautiously approached the nest. No Bumblebee. I quickly put the nest back on the clay dish, inverted the pot to cover it, put a cork in the opening (just in case she was still there) and screwed the whole thing back together. As I walked into the backyard to rehang the pot from the patio roof behind the garage, I saw the Bumblebee flying around the spot where her nest used to be. I took a deep breath and spoke to her gently. "I am sorry Bumblebee. I did not know this was your nest. I have put it all back together so let me hang it back up and you can have your nice, cozy home back. Just hold on for a few more seconds, OK? No stingy me, OK?" She backed up and let me hang her nest. As soon as it was up she flew inside. Home sweet home.

Later that day I was watching the news and saw a clip of Governor Chris Christy proudly smashing a Spider that had crawled onto a table in classroom he was visiting. The children cheered. Tears welled up in my eyes for that Spider, who was doing nothing more than walking towards its home. Tears also fell for the children, whose hearts were already hardened to the sacredness of life and, on that day, the tender life of the smallest creature.

How can some be so indifferent? It is no wonder we are killing this planet when we have taught our children to revel in the death of one so small.

The Soul of the Animals

Many humans like to believe that other animals don't feel emotion. Perhaps that makes it easier for us to kill, maim, injure, torture, use them in lab experiments, or eat them. If you knew the pain that a fish experiences when a hook rips into its mouth, would you still fish? Some would.

There are videos that show adult elephants mourning, returning to the place where one of their family or herd members died. They rock back and forth in an elephant funeral ritual. They mourn. They feel emotion.

Here is a story that will sound unbelievable, but I swear to you it is true...

When I lived in Pennsylvania I volunteered at a wildlife rehabilitation center were there lived variety of animals including bear cats, vultures, owls, and hawks. I helped to feed the animals and clean out their cages. The bear cats, a rare mammal from Madagascar, ate chopped vegetables. The birds ate small mice or rats, all frozen. Each day I would go into the freezer, grab a frozen white rat by the tail, take it into an owl pen, and place it in the food dish.

One day we started noticing an odor. It smelled of something rotten. We couldn't locate the source of the smell. Over the next several days the odor became more intense due to hot weather.

In the center of the building where the animals were housed was a large, square metal box with three-foot high sides and an open top. This was used to re-train the predatory birds to capture mice.

The smell was coming from under that box.

The owner started up her fork lift and drove it to the shiny box. Carefully she slid the forks under the box and slowly lifted it. Then, she backed up. I could not believe my eyes.

116

There, under that box, were hundreds of dead white rats. Bisecting the stacks of dead rats were linear pathways. It was a rat cemetery.

She turned off the fork lift and took her place next to me, staring in disbelief at what we were witnessing. Apparently, the resident rat population (living) were taking the bodies of their dead white rat comrades from the pens and placing them under the box. It was their cemetery, the place where they honored their dead. They did not know the white rats. But they cared for them anyway.

The owner bulldozed the pile of dead rats out into the woods. I felt sad for the rats. All of them.

Charlotte

Several times I have gotten ready to turn the water on in the bathtub in order to take a shower, only to stop myself in the nick of time before drowning a poor little ant or spider. Once or twice my hand turned the knob just a millisecond before my eyes spotted an ant desperately trying to climb up the slippery ceramic sides of the tub, and down the drain they went. I felt horrible.

Usually I will place a long piece of toilet paper draped across the bottom and over the side of the tub to serve as a "ladder" so any helpless little creature can climb out.

For the past few weeks there has been a particular spider, who I now call Charlotte, that has made several trips to the bottom of the tub. "On belay!" she cries as she lets her spinnerets do their thing. Down she goes, an invisible thread connecting her to the silk wisteria that borders the ceiling of my bathroom (hold your tongue). She finally lands in the bottom of the bath tub. And there she must stay until I rescue her.

"Hello Charlotte, jumping off cliffs again?" I ask, as I tear a small piece of toilet paper for her to crawl onto. Usually it takes a few tries before we figure out each other's moves, and Charlotte will disappear into the fluffy white folds. Up she goes until the elevator reaches the top floor of Wisteria Lane, and she will walk out onto one of the white silk flowers. "Now be careful, Charlotte!" I say. "One of these days I might miss you and you will either drown or starve to death!" She disappears in green leaves.

Charlotte and I are developing a relationship. Every time I go in the bathroom I search for her with my eyes. "Charlotte, how is your day?" I ask her. "Catch any little gnats?" "Are you warm enough?" I had closed the damper on the heating vent some time before I first met Charlotte, and realized it was mighty cold in there for a little spider. So, I opened it so she could be warm again. I know she appreciates it.

I have had several relationships with Spiders in my lifetime. Each one has been special. There is an ease to connecting with them, I am not sure why, given the bad rap they get. Every Spider I have ever known has had an open heart and welcomes a smile instead of a squish.

So next time you see Spider in your house, take a moment and just watch her. Get to know her. You will find your heart warmed by the experience. Seriously.

The Mysterious Bird

One morning I awoke slightly before sunrise, which is usual for me. It was summer, the time when robins start singing before dawn. I rolled to the side of my bed, swung my legs over and did my ritual stretch. The dog didn't move, still blissfully snoring away. I glanced at the digital numbers shining red in their dashes, the clock said two minutes before six. I went to the bathroom, brushed my teeth, and did other human bathroom things. But something caught my attention. I could hear a bird singing outside and it wasn't a robin. I followed the song which led me back into the bedroom. My window was cracked open and a beautiful melody flowed through the screen and up into my ears. I leaned downed and listened. Who was that?

It is true I am a biologist, but I have never become proficient in the language of birds. I know some bird calls of course and can converse quite fluently with Barred and Screech Owls, Sandhill Cranes, Mourning Doves, and Chickadees. But this song was totally unfamiliar to me. Maybe it was a migrant gone astray. Maybe it was an escaped pet. I shook my head and went on with my day.

The next morning, I heard this beautiful song again. This time I went out to the backyard to look for the mysterious visitor. It stopped singing. Must be a shy little thing, I thought. I waited and listened. Nothing. Shrugging my shoulders, I went back into the house. Wait, there it is again! I ran into my bedroom, leaned down to where the window was opened and listened. The bird was singing again!

I tried to memorize the call. I counted notes, I counted phrases. I tried to write the melody out. For several days I listened. The bird was only out around six o'clock in the morning, stopped singing when I went outside to find it, and was not native to this area. I was stumped.

I scoured the internet for bird calls. I listened to my recordings of bird calls. I finally spoke with a couple of ornithologists (bird experts) that I worked with about this unusual visitor. They didn't have a clue.

What struck me most about this bird was its punctuality. It always called around six in the morning, which was odd because the sunrise was well underway and most early birds would have been singing for at least an hour by then.

This was driving me crazy. I had never been stumped before on any animal identification.

I remember it was a Thursday. I heard that bird again. It was six o'clock on the dot. I leaned down over my night stand to the crack in the window to listen. I moved closer to the window. The bird seemed to get a bit quieter. Huh? I leaned back a little, the bird got a bit louder. I leaned down a little more and the bird got a bit louder. I leaned down further until my ear was directly over the Tranquil Sounds alarm clock radio sitting on my dresser.

The alarm, which went off at six o'clock, was set to rainforest.

God did I feel stupid.

Are Pigs Naturally Fat?

I was watching a rerun of Northern Exposure one morning, an episode about a mosquito festival and a truffle-sniffing pig, when I suddenly wondered if pigs were naturally fat. I remembered some photos I had seen a long time ago of laboratory rats that had been fed so much food they looked like grotesque hairy sausages. Seemed that they, like other animals, will eat and eat and eat if given an unlimited supply of food. For whatever reason, that truffle sniffing pig looked like a laboratory experiment to me. Grotesquely obese. What does a normal pig look like, one that is fit and trim?

According to Wikipedia, pig is any of the animals in the genus *Sus*, within the Suidae family of even-toed ungulates. Pigs include the domestic pig (*Sus scrofa domestica*), its ancestor the wild boar, and several other wild relatives. Pigs are omnivores and are highly social and intelligent animals. We are averse to eating other highly social and intelligent animals, so why do we put aside this aversion to gnaw on a pork chop? Pigs rank fourth in the list of most intelligent animals in the world, behind chimps, dolphins, and elephants. Who knew? They learn tricks faster than dogs and their grunts are a complex form of communication. They are very close to their mates. Pigs like to snuggle up with each other at night when they sleep, are very family oriented, and live in Tribes. Sounds like my kind of people.

Pigs don't have any sweat glands, so they don't like heat. That is why they have to roll around in the mud, to cool off. They are also fantastic swimmers. Whodda thunk?

To imagine what a healthy, fit pig would look like, I turn to the wild boar. Wild boars live a natural lifestyle, eat whatever they can find, and burn lots of calories doing so. They are lean and mean. Maybe that is it. Domestic pigs don't get much exercise so they gain weight. I can relate to that. I learned a baby pig eats so much its first week it actually doubles in weight! But I wasn't satisfied with this crumb of information, I needed more.

So, I searched the internet and asked the question "why are pigs fat?" Turns out they aren't. Pigs are giant, muscle-bound animals with small legs, making them appear to be portly. Just shows you can't judge a book by its cover. I learned many things while researching Pigs and we are a lot like each other. Highly social and very intelligent.

I am sure I will think twice before biting into the next piece of bacon.

My Friend

Every few years I get ambitious and go after the "weeds" that start to grow in my raspberry patch, grape arbor, and lily of the valley garden. One time, while pulling up a plant, I noticed a Snake skin. Upon further searching, I found several more. Seems Snake found the perfect spot to shed her skin.

It didn't take long before Snake showed herself to me, a beautiful Garter. I called her Elizabeth and looked for her every time I worked in the yard. Sometimes she was by the compost pile, sometimes she draped herself on the stack of apple tree branches pruned during the winter. One day, Elizabeth was sunning herself with a friend, a smaller Garter. They were beautiful.

A few years passed and Elizabeth moved on. I missed her.

This spring, a Snake a bit smaller than Elizabeth showed up in the backyard. She loved to spend her time within the piles of straw blanketing the ground under the McIntosh apple tree. It was cool and damp there, desirable conditions for snakes such as she. I named her Gracie.

I had to be careful when walking in the yard because this little one loved to sun herself between the little white clovers that I leave growing for the bees. She also loved the shade of the holly trees, where sweet drips of water could be found at the faucet.

These past few weeks have had record setting temperatures here in my town, from the nineties to over one hundred degrees. A taste of what we have done to our atmosphere, a glimpse of what our summers will be like from now on. I see the animals struggling to find places of coolness. Squirrels in the bird bath. Robins in the sprinklers.

I have been diligent about keeping two sources of water filled for my animal and insect neighbors. I run the sprinkler for a little while, several times a day so the birds and squirrels can cool off, and the grass can stay green for the rabbits to eat. And I hose down the straw for Snake, so she can stay cool in her dark hideaway.

This morning I answered a knock at the door. After stating her business, the woman said, "Do you know you have a snake on your front side walk?" "No," I replied and stepped outside. "It is there in the mulch, coiled up. I think it is dead."

I walked a few feet down the concrete path and looked down. There, freshly molted, was the most beautiful snake I had ever seen. My friend Gracie. She had deep rich colors of green and blue adjacent to beautiful cream-colored stripes. Gracie was loosely coiled up, her mouth wide open and bright red. My friend was dead.

There were no signs of injury. Just a beautiful healthy-looking Garter snake.

My heart sank. I felt a deep sadness, a tremendous loss. I had watched out for her, provided her water, tried to keep her straw pile cool in the intense heat wave. I admired her beauty, I talked with her while watering the garden. I looked for her each time I went out in the yard. And now she was gone.

I picked her body up and placed her under the beautiful pink rose bush, saying a prayer taught to me by Grandma Twylah. And I wondered how many more snakes and birds and squirrels and fawns died today from something that I and all other humans helped create. I feel such deep sorrow for the suffering that climate change is causing the other Beings that share this planet with us. Snake was the first casualty I witnessed firsthand and that makes it all the more real.

My heart is still heavy with sadness knowing that tomorrow will come without my Snake friend. It will bring with it another day of extreme heat, and I don't know what to do to help my friends.

Ear Wigs

I know there are many people who get the creepy crawlies from the creepy crawlies. Insects. Oh, they may marvel at a butterfly, the glamorous poster child of the insect world. But the rest? They get stepped on, squished, obliterated, fumigated, and berated.

Ever heard the saying "sticks and stones may break my bones but words will never hurt me?" Names are words, and I can't think of too many names that evoke disgust and repulsion like Earwig. OK, maybe Tick and Leech are right up there. But this is the year of the Earwig.

The name is blamed on an old wives' tale that Earwig burrowed into the brains of humans through the ear and laid their eggs. Wikipedia tells us that Earwigs are predisposed to hiding in warm humid crevices and may indeed occasionally crawl into the human ear canal (much like any other small organism). I don't know about you, but I have never heard of anyone I know having an Earwig crawl into their ear. Have you? Fodder for gossip, I say. Another attempt to malign Earwigs. Balderdash!

Earwigs are nocturnal and they often hide in small, moist crevices during the day. They are omnivorous and enjoy eating insects (mostly Arthropods) and plants. Here's something else you might not know, many species of Earwigs display maternal instincts, caring for the young little Earwigs until they reach the age of two (molts).

Isn't that sweet? Not only that, some Orders of Earwigs actually have live births (as opposed to laying eggs). Now I bet you didn't know that, either.

The common Earwig we have in Michigan was introduced from Europe in 1907. We do have a native species, but it is very secretive and seldom seen.

I once bought a very interesting straw hat one day and hosed it down and set it out in the sun to dry. Late that afternoon, I went

126

to a party with my fancy new hat perched on top of my head. Whilst leaving the party, I felt a bite on my forehead. "Ouch!" I exclaimed. I instinctively reached up to brush my attacker away. It was an Earwig! I was pinched by an Earwig! I felt honored. I felt initiated. I felt blessed to be chosen by this particular Earwig. It dropped to the porch floor and scampered away to find some deep, dark crevice in which to hide.

So, the next time you see an Earwig scurrying across the basement floor, remember it could be a Mother trying to find one of her cute little babies. Let her go and feel blessed to share your space with such fascinating and misunderstood creatures.

How Can We Not Love?

Soft bud emerging into a world of grays and browns
opening and unfolding into the freshest green
giving the gift of oxygen and shade
and brilliant colors in their death
How can we not love the leaves?

Cool flowing creek filled with crayfish and trout
formed from raindrops that fell from the sky
merging with others forming rivers
that carry canoes and feed the world
How can we not love the waters?

Dragonfly perched on moss-covered log
Sunlight reflecting the colors of the
Rainbow off translucent iridescent wings
Fairies of the woods and ponds
How can we not love the dragonfly?

Sandhill cranes in field with their young
long legs walking, step, step
outstretched wings flapping, lifting, lifting
three beautiful birds take flight
How can we not love the cranes?

Polar bear walks on snow
large paw prints trailing behind majestic and regal
slides into sea
a ghost bear in a blue ocean
How can we not love the bear?

Salmon going home
swims its last swim
to lay eggs to give life
in her death
How can we not love the salmon?

Sunsets and the northern lights

Oceans and lakes, rivers and streams
Mountains and valleys
Prairies and deserts
Tundra and ice caps
Forests and fields
How can we not love the Earth?

Mining and drilling into her body,
toxins released into her waters
oil spills sealing the fates of millions
devouring the last wild places we know
Why can we not love ourselves?

The Crow

A couple of days ago I was milling around the house when I heard a ruckus in the backyard. The kind of ruckus that sends shivers up the spine. It was the frantic and panic-filled cries of my robins, the ones that built a nest in my apple tree. And rising from the middle of the shrill alarm calls was the high-pitched cry of a baby bird.

I don't watch nature shows because I can't stand the killing. I know it is part of the cycle of life but it bothers the heck out of me. I know the predator must eat. But god does it have to be so violent? And now in digital?

I raced to the backyard, hoping to interrupt what I knew would be a National Geographic moment. But I was too late. Bursting from the tree branch which held the beautiful mud-lined robin nest flew a crow. In its talons was a baby robin, wings flapping wildly, little voice calling for help in high pitched notes. The parents made a valiant attempt to rescue their baby, but the crow flew off into the trees with a pair of fluffy little black wings flapping frantically in its clutches. I should have stayed indoors.

Mama robin perched herself on the telephone line that hangs a few feet south of her nest. I walked up to her, and in the softest voice I could muster, told her how sorry I was that she had lost her baby. She had a look of disorientation in her eye, not the peaceful, secure, strong gaze I was used to seeing. She was grieving. I stayed with her for several minutes, assuring her I would keep the beagle in the backyard more often and that I would keep the hose on alert for the next time crow decided to come dining.

Later that evening, I heard the chirping of baby birds and watched as mama robin fed her two remaining offspring. Their enormous mouths, which emerged from small fuzzy heads, bobbed up and down above the stick edges of the nest. I searched the trees for the crow, hose in hand and beagle on patrol. Bellies full, the little birds snuggled in for a bird nap.

I slept better that night knowing my birds were safe. But geez it is hard to be Godmother to a nest full of baby robins in a world full of crows.

Lost in the Poconos

Early October can be cold in the Pocono Mountains of Pennsylvania, especially after the sun goes down. It is also the time when some of the rare moths appear. Here then, is the tale of being lost in the Poconos one late October night.

We were driving along the winding mountain roads searching for obscure pull-offs where we could park the car and walk into the woods unnoticed. Our objective was to look for good spots to put out black light traps, which are used to attract moths. We had explored about five potential trap sites when the sun began to set. I looked up into the sky and saw the first stars of the night. The constellation Cassiopeia was beginning to appear. Just beautiful.

"Let's check this one out," said fellow biologist Charles. "OK," I said, and we hopped out of the car and made our way into the woods, boots crunching on the dry leaves. After traveling about fifty yards or so, we decided to head back to the car. We turned around and walked back the way we came. We walked and we walked. There was no car, no pull-off.

"Where are we?" I asked. "The car should be right here!" "I don't know," he responded. "Let's keep looking."

The battery on my headlamp, the only light we had, was beginning to die as the fading light bounced off the trees. I was starting to shiver, as I had not worn a coat. Every exhale produced a cloud of vapor. We walked for half an hour and still no sign of the car. Cassiopeia continued to shine above us.

"We should build a fire," Charles said. "I don't think so Charles, I think we should build a survival shelter so that we can keep warm until morning." Back and forth we went as we peered into the darkness, looking for a glimmer of hope in the form of light shining on a bumper.

"OK, hold on," I said. I pulled out the topographical map.

"Listen and look Charles. Do you hear the sound of this highway?" I asked, pointing to the major roadway indicated on the map. "It is coming from over there," I said. "I have been watching the stars all night, and if I can find a clearing so that I can see Cassiopeia clearly, I think I can figure out where we are using this map. We have been gone for a couple of hours and I think she should have shifted about this far in the sky during that time. She came up in the east." I held my hand up to the sky, making two inches between my thumb and index finger.

We searched the heavily forested area until finally coming into a small clearing. There, through the branches of an oak tree, shined Cassiopeia. Orienting myself to this beautiful constellation and to the sound of the highway, I calculated a route that would take us back to the road we came in on. We might not find the car, but at least we would have a road.

Charles thought I was crazy. I knew better.

Our boots shuffled through the leaves as we walked in the direction that Cassiopeia sent us. Within fifteen minutes, the dim light of my headlamp reflected off the bumper of a car. Our car.

Ever since I was a young girl I have known to pay attention to my surroundings. I look at the trees, the plants, the slope of the hill, what stars are out and where they are in the sky. How high was the sun, how high is the sun now? Does it smell like rain? What kind of soil am I walking on? Dry sand, or dark organics, indicating a former wetland? What birds are singing? I don't use GPS when in the woods or in the car. I want to be connected in my body and Spirit to the world around me. I don't want to be lost when that rechargeable battery dies.

But most importantly, I don't want to miss one bit of the glory of Nature that surrounds me. Not one bit.

A Life Lost

One of the things that every field biologist has thought of at least once in their professional life is finding a dead body. After all, we are out in every nook and cranny - from the beautiful wilderness to the urban rivers. Of all the biologists I know, I am the only one who has actually found one.

I remember the day. It was a hot morning in April. I worked for the city of Ann Arbor as a lepidopterist, surveying for butterflies in the many beautiful parks. That particular day I was visiting an undeveloped area on the outskirts of town. I pulled my old Honda Accord off the road into a rough parking area, got out, and opened the trunk. I pulled on my rubber hip waders, put on my field vest, binoculars, hat, fanny pack, and camera, grabbed my butterfly net and shut the trunk. Down the old two track I went headed toward the first stop of the day, a pretty little meadow in the middle of a forest.

After searching the small, sunlit clearing for skippers, I made my way through a tangle of downed logs and heavy brush and popped out into the marsh. It was always slow going, but on some days, there was a bit of standing water which actually exerted pressure on the bottom muck and made it more solid and easier to walk through. Other days it was pretty soupy and it was all you could do to keep your balance, let alone chase after something with wings.

I followed my usual route through the wetland and was headed in the general direction of my car when I noticed something blue off in the distance. "A five-gallon bucket," I thought and kept going. As I got closer, the blue bucket turned into a pile of trash, or at least that is what it looked like through all the shrubs and vegetation. At first, I was a bit angry at the person who dumped their garbage into this park. But then I realized that in order to get the trash to that spot someone would have had to get out of their car and walk through the marsh. Not likely.

I was making my way teetering and tottering through the muck and the hummocks when I came upon an odor I will never forget. And at the same time the odor wafted into my nostrils, my eyes fell upon the body of a man.

At first, I was terrified. I didn't know if he was drunk or passed out. I thought, "How can I get away in these hip waders with all this gear hanging off me?" But then I saw the flies and I knew he was dead. Time seemed to stand still for a moment, then slowly start up again in slow motion. I knew from being a former fan of CSI and Law and Order that I should stay away from the body in case it was a crime scene. I pulled my cell phone out and called the police.

Once the police arrived I had to stay within the taped-off crime scene area while they investigated. Hours and hours. When I was finally cleared to go, I left the scene and went to a friend's house.

A few days later I found out the man, only twenty-eight years old, had committed suicide.

According to his family, he had been despondent and was missing for the two weeks prior to his death. Had I not been there looking for butterflies, there was a good chance his body would not have been found for months or years or maybe never. No one went out into this marsh. No one except for me and him. I was glad to have found him, for his family's sake. How horrible to never know what happened to a missing loved one.

I had to go back to that very same place the following week and was anxious and uncomfortable. I knew that finding his body had deeply affected me on many levels. I was startled by any human-made object that didn't belong in nature. I was saddened that this person had felt so hopeless he ended his life.

I took a bunch of flowers with me and walked directly out to the spot where he had died. I stood there holding the blossoms and looked around, seeing what he saw in his last minutes, wondering how he felt. In the last moments of consciousness, as the drugs made their way through his body, did he regret it? Did he try to get out of the marsh and go for help? Did he feel relief? Or did he feel nothing at all? I looked down at the spot where his body had lain down on the Earth. He was facing an old weeping willow tree. Did he look at the tree? Did the tree hear his final words or cries? Was the willow now weeping for him?

I have known depression. Intimately. I have felt the deep hopelessness and despair that comes with this horrible and debilitating condition. I have wanted to give up, to end the suffering in my heart. And I tried once and failed. He tried and he succeeded. He had been there to show me what suicide looks like to those left behind. It is final. It is the end.

All hope vanishes with the Spirit of the departed. I placed my bouquet of flowers where he last lay and said a prayer to his Spirit and to the Creator. I prayed for the land, which holds all memory. I prayed for his family who would have years of heartache from this terrible tragedy.

I don't know how to end this story, except to say that no matter what, there is always hope. Even if we can't see it. Depression is unbearable at times, it can wear you out and take you to the end of your rope. But there is always hope if we want a better life. As someone once said, "Don't drop anchor here." Sadly, he did.

Mushroom Hunting Disorder (MHD)

Grandma was at the top of the stairs, greeting me as she always did. Her driveway wound itself around to the backside of "the mound", where I would enter the house through the basement door and walk up the carpeted steps into her loving arms. After a big hug and a kiss, Grandma took my hand and said "Come here, I want to show you something."

Hand in hand we walked through the kitchen, stepped out into the screened-in porch, and exited via the side door. Gravel crunched under Grandma's small, well-worn tennis shoes as she led me to a carefully stacked column of three little pieces of limestone gravel.

"Look what I found," she proudly said.

Beside the tiny monument was a black morel.

Ah, a black morel, the object of my obsession. Grandma's yard was always full of black morels. Some springs were better than others, but most of the time I could count on them to bring me bliss. I would stand at Grandma's kitchen sink and look out her large picture window, searching the green grass for protruding objects. Past the bird feeding station, down the hill to the old burn pile my eyes would travel. I could pick out a morel at fifty yards if the light was right. Grandma mostly ignored them, unless I called her and asked for a report. For some reason, on that day, she went hunting.

Hello, my name is Barb B. and I have MHD. MHD (Mushroom Hunting Disorder) is an obsessive/compulsive disorder yet to be included in the Physicians' Desk Reference. Hereditary in nature, it was passed on to me from my parents, who got it from their parents, who got it from their parents. My case seems to be the worst the family has ever seen. Symptoms include sleep disturbance, obsessive thoughts, inability to focus, impaired driving (due to looking for mushrooms while operating vehicle), and compulsive lying. It most commonly occurs in people living in Michigan, although in recent years it has spread to surrounding states. There appears to be two forms of this disorder. Out-of-state visitors tend to be obsessed more with profits than mushrooms. Michigan residents are obsessed more with mushrooms.

My disorder begins its cycle in February, when my sleep becomes disturbed by dreams of morels...fields of giant white morels that are the prize of all mushroom hunters. The dreams continue until the trilliums appear, at which time I am drawn by some unseen force into the woods. I cannot help myself, I cannot stop myself. I must find mushrooms.

I began to hunt morels when I was knee high to a grasshopper. Since then, I have learned many more species of mushrooms and my obsession lasts until the first snow flies. Usually the cycle ended at the start of winter and I would have relief for a few months. Now, I have become acquainted with chaga the birch fungus which can be harvested year around. I have no peace.

It is only March, and already I have been out seeking fungus. I went to my old haunts and there, growing on a dead log, were baby dryad saddles. I pulled out my knife. "No!" I screamed to myself, "Not the children!" I bit my lip and kept walking. Soon, I found some teenage dryad's saddles. The perfect size. Using my mushroom knife, which is characterized by its extremely sharp, curved blade and wooden handle with a compass on the side and a brush on the end, I sliced several of the mushrooms and reverently placed them in my bag. The season had begun.

Now I cannot concentrate. I watch the weather. I worry and get filled with anxiety if I see someone walking in the woods behind my house. Are they looking for Morels? I grab my coat and walk as fast as I can to get around them undetected. I go into the woods and crouch low, searching the ground for those rare jewels of spring. If I find mushrooms I will lie to anyone who asks. I will say I did not find anything. Nothing. Nada.

I never lie. Ever. Except when it comes to mushrooms.

Blessed Honeybees

Last year I discovered that I had lost both my bee hives. One colony died of starvation, they weren't able to store enough honey to carry them through the winter. The other perished from Colony Collapse Disorder. They simply vanished, leaving behind a hive full of honey.

I bought two more packages of bees and put them in the hives last one May. We spent the summer getting to know each other, and over the following winter I went out to check on them, putting on a stethoscope and listening to each hive for the low-pitched hum. The ancient practice of bee shamanism contains many secrets of beekeeping. Things like the little-known fact that bees love to hear stories. So, I told them stories. I sang them songs. I prayed that they would survive into spring. And they did.

It was the first warm day of the season and the girls were out in full force. In the winter on warm days they will take "elimination" flights, I am sure you can figure that out. But these new flights had a greater purpose. They were foraging.

I look outside my big picture window and I see the naked landscape, no longer winter and not quite yet spring. The snowdrops are blooming in my backyard and the red maple trees have donned their blossoms. But that is all I can see of spring.

The bees, however, see much more. I was surprised to observe the girls flying in with large pollen sacs on their back legs, they had found flowers! And they must have found lots of them, because almost every other bee entering the hive was weighted down with large white bundles of protein-rich pollen. And with that pollen they bring nectar to make honey. Spring has truly arrived.

I have two bee hives, a traditional Langstroth box and a newer top-bar hive. I noticed fewer bees going in and out of the top-bar, so since it was a nice warm day I decided to open it up and check on the girls.

Using a metal pry bar, I gently lifted each frame and marveled at the beautiful, free hanging honey comb. The newest was ivory white, this year's comb. They artfully build two heart-shaped combs side by side, then connect them, creating one large comb. Honeybees hold on to each other's legs and form bee chains to measure by. Simply amazing.

All seemed well in the bee hive, with some combs beginning to be filled with brood as indicated by the raised cap on the cell of the comb. Many combs were glowing with honey, that sweet, sacred liquid treasured by all. I asked the girls if I might have one comb, and after much bee discussion, they agreed. I cut the comb from the wooden top bar and placed it on a fine screen that seats nicely on my five-gallon honey bucket. Mashing the comb with a wooden spoon, the smell of fresh honey filled my kitchen almost immediately. Pearls of golden ambrosia began to drip into the bucket.

It takes five million flowers to make one pint of honey. This morning I filled my mason jars with ten and a half million flowers worth. Mind blowing. Blessed honeybees.

Fish Don't Swim Backwards

I used to love ice fishing. Oh, the joy of getting all bundled up in my snowmobile suit and Sorels, schlepping a five-gallon plastic bucket filled with my short little ice fishing pole, tackle box, bait, and that long spoon thingy with the holes in it across the freezing ice tundra. You know, the spoon thingy that you dip into the water in the hole you drilled to lift out the ice? I'd hoist the old steel ice auger with the spoon on the end over my shoulder, be sure I had my pretzel rods and a beer or two in my bulky pockets, and off I would go out onto the ice. Crunch, crunch, crunch went my boots as I made my way to the spot I hoped would bring me luck.

One day I got the bright idea of taking a tip-up with me. For those of you who have never ice fished, a tip-up is best described as a wooden frame with a small orange flag that sits over a hole in the ice. When a fish bites, usually a big fish, the flag "tips up" to let you know you've caught one. I thought maybe I could catch a pike, so I took it along just in case. That particular day I went out by myself and set up at a favorite perch spot.

Using the cold steel auger, I bored a hole in the ice, set my bucket upside down next to it, and put some bait on my hook. I used the spoon thingy to remove the ice that was beginning to form on the surface of the water in the hole and dropped my line into the darkness. It wasn't long before I saw the bobber disappear, and I pulled out the first perch, a nice one. I took the perch off the hook, put it in a bucket, and reset my line. After about a half hour of pulling perch out of the dark depths of the lake, I decided to try the tip-up.

I should have known this was not a good idea. First, I had to bait the hook, and the bait was a large fat minnow. A chub I think it was called. I did not like that one bit. After saying I was sorry a hundred times to that little fish, I tossed the baited line into the second hole, set the flag on the tip-up, and went back to the first hole to fish for more perch.

Not five minutes after I sat down the flag popped up.

I jumped up and began to reel in whatever was on the other end. And I thought of that poor minnow. I must say I was excited and a bit scared all at the same time. This was my first solo ice fishing trip. I had never used a tip up before. I didn't know what to expect. It wasn't long before I pulled the large fish up out of the hole. It was Pike.

Pike was huge. Like twenty-four inches long or maybe she was three feet, I don't know. But she was big. And she had teeth. I had caught a pike before while trolling the lake at night, but for some reason on this day it was like I realized for the first time pike had teeth.

I also realized my Dad wasn't with me. I didn't like to take fish off the hook. Dad would do that for me. I was ok with the smaller fish, but if I were to catch a bigger fish like bass, or salmon on the big lake, well I turned that task over to him. Now, here I was on this stark, cold, barren lake. Alone. With a big pike. With teeth.

"Ok," I thought to myself. "Now what?" I had to get the hook out of her mouth. I had to touch her. I reached down, and got real close, but I just couldn't do it. Damn! "Ok, Barb, don't be a wimp. You can do this." Always creative, I took my stocking cap off, put it on the fish, got out my pliers, and successfully removed the hook from Pike's mouth. Whew.

Now what do I do with her? I could put her in the bucket and take her back with me, but I am sure she will flop out of the bucket and onto the seat of my car and then into the front seat only to bite me. No, that would not work. "I know," I said to no one. "If I let the fish lay here on the ice surely she will freeze to death and not be able to bite me." I looked at that poor fish there on the ice and immediately decided to return her home. So, I took my heavy Sorel boot and pushed Pike back into the hole.

Backwards.

I watched as Pike bobbed up and down. Why wasn't she swimming away, I wondered? Then I realized. Fish don't swim backwards. Duh.

So now I am watching this mouth full of teeth bobbing up and down, and realized I have to take her out of the water once again, turn her around, and slide her back down the hole head first. Great.

I took my pliers and grabbed Pike by the mouth and pulled her up out of the hole. After Pike quit flopping around on the ice, I turned her around and scooted her once again with my Sorel boot, this time head first into the hole. I watched as Pike gratefully disappeared into the darkness.

I've often wondered about Pike and whether she lived a long and healthy life, telling all the little Pikes about the time she traveled to the top of the world and back again. I am sure the moral of the story is always the same, a warning to the little Pikelettes.

There is no such thing as a free lunch.

Wing Prints in Snow

Large snowflakes drifted steadily from the cold, gray sky, kissing my cheeks before melting away. I lay on the ground in the barren winter field, cheeks red and cold, but bundled warm and snug in my black snowmobile suit with the yellow stripes down the sleeves. From where did Snow come from, I wondered? I tried to focus on a single Snowflake as far up as I could see and watch its journey downward alongside millions of its sisters and brothers. The view reminded me of those scenes on Star Trek, where the Enterprise is traveling at Warp speed through the galaxy, stars whizzing by. I was thirteen years old.

Childlike wonder and excitement fill my heart when Snow first covers the ground. It is my favorite holiday, the First Snowfall, the most magical day of the year. It is a time of peace, when I feel safer somehow, comforted. That winter blanket keeps me snug and warm, no matter what is going on in my world.

It was a cold, crisp, blue-sky winter morning when I walked into the woods one February day searching for signs of Fox. There was a light dusting of powdery Snow on top of a thin, crusty layer of ice, which sparkled like tiny diamonds in the sunlight. Snow crunched under my boots as I made my way into a small grove of young trees.

I began to follow tracks of Mouse where it hopped through the snow. I knew the little creature had walked here sometime during the night as the tracks were fresh and clear. Mouse would go from tree to tree, circling each before moving to the next. But then, the tracks disappeared. Vanished in mid- trail. There, on either side of the last pair of tracks, were wing prints.

As I made my way through the woods, I saw evidence of this night time drama playing out over half a dozen times. Mouse tracks running from tree to tree, circling the trunks, then disappearing, the last tracks framed by wing prints. Because of the distance between the wing tips and the fact there were only the tips of the wings showing in the snow, this must have been the work of Screech Owls. I imagined them quietly gliding through the woods, snatching up unsuspecting Mice from the snow. I am sure the Owls were well-fed that night.

Soon I found the tracks of Fox and followed them as they wound their way through a field, in and out of dried Goldenrod stems and Asters. There I could see a tunnel where Meadow Vole had pushed up the snow as it made its way along a little trail. I noticed where Fox had stopped and poked its nose into Vole's tunnel, perhaps checking to see if anyone was home. There were tracks of Rabbit, too, and signs of their feeding on wild Raspberry stalks. Rabbits are unusual in that they have two pairs of front teeth, one behind the other. When biting off a stem or a twig, they leave behind a cut as clean as if made with the blade of a sharp knife. Deer, on the other hand, have no upper front teeth and leave a jagged stem behind.

I slowly and quietly followed Fox's trail up a small rise, and as I crested the hill, I saw a glimpse of orange there in the dried weeds. It was Fox, curled up in the warm sun, taking a morning nap. I stood and marveled at its beauty, and then quietly retreated, leaving Fox to its dreams. Yes, winter is indeed the most magical time of year.

Trapped by Pride

There is a cave in Pennsylvania called Nails 2. How it got its name I do not know. To find Nails 2, one wanders through the woods looking for a small, triangular-shaped hole in the ground a little bigger than a football. To enter Nails 2 requires descending a twenty-five-foot vertical shaft on a six-inch-wide cable ladder. For those unfamiliar with cable ladders, they are two pieces of thin steel cable with aluminum steps the size of a #2 pencil.

Our mission was to survey this remote cave for rare invertebrates that live in the cold subterranean waters. Brandon was my intern, a short but fit young guy who came from a family of horse jockeys. We suited up, put on our caving helmets and gear bags, and prepared to enter the cave that most people over twenty-five refuse to enter. I was thirty-seven. We dropped the cable ladder down the small, dark hole. Brandon wriggled into the tight space and made his way down the ladder, reaching the first small room which was the size of a large gym locker. He yelled up for me to enter.

At that time, I was five feet eight and a half inches tall and weighed a good one hundred and sixty pounds. I was fit, but I did not come from a family of horse jockeys. I am sure you know where this is going.

I sat down in the dry leaves at the edge of that small, triangular-shaped hole in the ground. Feet first I stepped onto the ladder and down I went. I had descended about fifteen feet when I came to a pinch in the passage. No matter how hard I tried, I could not get below that pinch. Well, I was not about to be shown up by a punk nineteen-year-old intern, so I climbed up out of the cave, stripped off my caving suit and sweatshirt, and re-entered Nails 2, my diameter reduced by several inches. Again, I reached the pinch, and again I could not get past it. Common sense be damned! I exhaled as hard as I could and finally my mud-covered body slipped through. Victory!

Brandon and I stood compressed into that small first room,

contemplating the next drop which would take us to the main passage of the cave. To get there, we had to squeeze into another twenty-five-foot vertical drop that is best described as two stone walls facing each other, a foot apart. I looked at that large crack, looked at my thigh, and thought "my thigh is bigger than that crack". There was no way I would fit down that drop, even if I removed my remaining t-shirt and shorts. Brandon, of course, would have no trouble wriggling down into the depths of the unknown.

"You go on ahead" I said. "I am going back up and I'll wait for you on top". For safety, Brandon waited for me to climb out before continuing his descent. I put my foot onto the cable ladder, pulled myself up, and began the arduous task of climbing twenty-five feet to the surface through a hole not much bigger than my body.

I came to the infamous pinch. I couldn't get through. I tried again. And again. And again. I still could not get through. Exhausted, I climbed back down the ladder, and rested against the cold stone wall. We decided that Brandon would go on down to the stream at the bottom of the cave and search for invertebrates, and I would wait for him in the stone gym locker. He would then climb out of the cave, drop a rope, and pull me out. I watched him descend into the darkness. Then there was silence. I was alone.

For thirty minutes I stood in that cold, cramped space, occasionally looking up at the tiny patch of blue that reminded me of where I was. I couldn't get out. Panic started to grip me, squeezing my chest. I swear the walls started to close in. I knew if I let this go on I would risk my life and Brandon's...people who panic underground often never get out alive. So, I began to search for bugs. I searched every inch of that stone tomb for anything I could find, trying to keep thoughts of being trapped out of my head. Finally, I heard sounds from below and Brandon appeared. I was never so glad to see another human being in all my life.

He climbed up the cable ladder, his small body passing through the pinch with ease. Soon a climbing rope dropped down the hole and I tied it around my chest. "Pull!" I shouted up to Brandon. I started to climb the cable ladder, Brandon pulling hard on the rope. Halfway up, I reached the pinch again. "Pull hard!" I yelled. I felt the rope go taught, digging into my armpits. I pushed with all my might, but I could not get through. "Hold on!" I shouted. I rested for a few minutes, and we began again, pulling and pushing, trying to get me through the pinch.

By this time, I was so exhausted my entire body was shaking. I was sweaty, muddy, and my boots could not get a grip against the slick walls of this ungodly shaft into the netherworld. I was defeated. "Brandon!" I yelled up to the little blue triangle. "This is my last try! I can't go on". Oh god. He is going to have to go get the Cave Rescue Group. I will be in the papers, I will become infamous, a legend in the stories of the caving grottos. The thirty-seven-year old woman who took off all her clothes in order to cram her too large body into a hole that a woodchuck would avoid simply because she couldn't be shown up by her nineteen-year-old assistant. Oh god.

"You can do it!" Brandon yelled encouragingly down the little blue triangle. "One, two, three PULL!!!!!" I hollered. And I pushed with all my might. There was no way in hell I was going to be the subject of after-caving Pennsylvania diner talks. After all, I had my pride to consider. Oh wait; wasn't that what got me here in the first place? I pushed with my legs, I pulled with my arms, and Brandon pulled on the rope, and finally I made it past the pinch. A rush of relief engulfed me. I rested for a while before climbing the rest of the way out, and collapsed onto the ground, tired but free.

I hope that when mud-covered cavers gather for their hot buffet at the local diner after a long day of caving, they remember the tale of the woman who climbed into Nails 2 and made it out alive. A little more humble, but alive.

CHAPTER 6

ALASKA

The Gray Jay and the Pork Chop

It must have been day eight or so of a ten-day and two-night road trip to Alaska. We had stopped for lunch at a Provincial park somewhere in the Northwest Territory of Canada and were cooking barbequed pork chops under a beautiful northern sky. As I plated the last chop, I noticed a gray jay feeding on the dead insects stuck in the grill of the van. A photo op if I ever saw one.

I put my delicious pork chop on my plate along with all the side fixings and set it down on the old wooden picnic table. Quickly grabbing my Pentax ME Super, I walked slowly toward the van so as not to scare the jay. I focused the frame tightly on the bird as it nibbled on an unfortunate dragonfly. From one bug to the next the jay hopped eagerly, munching on a smorgasbord of beetles, moths, butterflies, dragonflies, and other mangled bodies. But there was something interesting about this jay. I swear I saw it looking at me in between hops.

All of a sudden, the jay flew faster than a jet over to the picnic table, grabbed my barbequed pork chop and flew off to the far side of the campsite. The bird and my delicious pork chop landed in the dirt twenty feet away. Of course, I kept snapping pictures and we watched that jay devour what was to be one of the best meals of the trip. We stared each other down that bird and I, and I swear it winked at me before flying away.

Gear, Kayaks, and the Alaska Candy Exchange

When I went back to college in the early 1980s, I decided to enroll in the electrical engineering program, due in no small part to pressure from my family and the fact I come from a long line of engineers. One of the core classes was general biology and lucky for me the professor's wife was a PhD candidate in wildlife biology. I had never heard of that field before and could not believe one could work in a job like that! I switched majors straight away. They took me under their wing and I eventually ended up at Michigan State University to pursue a degree in Fisheries and Wildlife Management. I had found my calling.

In my junior year, I saw a poster about the School for Field Stories on a bulletin board and was captivated by the beautiful pictures of Alaska advertising a course in marine mammal biology in Prince William Sound. I had always wanted to go to Alaska and the thought of living in the wild for nearly a month thrilled me. Through generous donations from friends and family, I was able to enroll and began my preparations.

Soon I received a thick packet of information in the mail from the school and devoured it in my excitement. We were given a list of items to bring and told that if we deviated from the list those items would be left behind. No Gore-Tex raingear was allowed, it had to be PVC-coated since we would be out during the rainy season. Knee-high rubber boots - yes. Down sleeping bags - no, they would get wet and never keep us dry and warm. Yes to wool socks, no to cotton. And on it went. The information said we would be paddling two-person fiberglass ocean kayaks for two hundred miles, so we were instructed to begin a regime of daily pushups to get our arms in shape. No less than thirty a day. No problem, I thought.

It took ten days and two nights to get to Alaska by car. That in and of itself was an adventure.

We finally arrived in Anchorage and the time had come to meet my class. We were a diverse group of fifteen students, a professor, her assistant, and an intern. Dr. Suzanne Marcy was an energetic and amazing young professor who specialized in Steller sea lions. Vernon Tejas, Suzanne's assistant, was a wild and crazy wilderness guide who relocated to Alaska from the lower forty-eight to work on the pipeline. He later became the first person to climb Denali solo in the winter and has since set many more climbing records around the world. And he yodeled pretty darn well. Intern Carmen was more serious in her demeanor and used her outdoor experience to make sure camp ran smoothly. Both were seasoned veterans of the Alaskan wilderness.

We all met at the Puffin Inn in Anchorage on July 25th, 1985. Staff went through the slow process of inventorying all our gear to make sure we packed only what we needed. I think I ended up leaving $200-$300 worth of gear behind! One last trip to the grocery store to pick up a few more food items and we were good to go. The kayaks and gear had been loaded onto the train so off we went along the Cook Inlet to Whittier.

After a scenic ride along the most beautiful tidal mud flat, we arrived in Whittier and began unloading all our gear. Other tourists that were already in town were very interested in what we were doing. It must have been quite a site, all those kayaks stacked up on the train. This small fishing town had a population of around three hundred people and used to be a military base. The entire population lived in an old military building that looked like a big apartment building and I could hear folks yelling out the windows to their neighbors. The smell of salt and fish lingered in the air. In the port, there was a harbor where many fishing boats were docked. In the distance, you could see Lion Island, a piece of dark colored rock jutting up through the ocean which looked like, you guessed it, a lion. We made camp and settled in to prepare for our trip the next day.

This was blackfly season so we had to wear head nets the moment we stepped off the train. The nets became a regular part of our morning dressing ritual. Those little blackfly buggers would bite you without you knowing it. Then a big welt would appear and it would itch and hurt. Back then I didn't know how bad DEET was for you (I learned later after accidently spilling some on a pair of binoculars, which immediately melted the coating) so I oiled up well to protect other exposed areas of my body.

Finally, it was time to learn how to paddle the boats. Most of us had never kayaked before, although I was an experienced canoeist so I wasn't too worried. First, we received a demonstration on how to pack the gear into the boats, using our paddles to shove things to the very front of the kayak. We were carrying everything we needed for twenty-five days in the wild, including fuel, stoves, food, clothes, tents, tarps, raingear, and cameras. That was a lot of stuff to fit in a kayak and we had to pack the gear of two people into each boat plus our bodies! I quickly learned that touching the inside of the fiberglass kayak with bare skin was not a good thing, the fibers would work their way into my skin and sting.

Once we had the boats packed, the next item on the agenda was learning how to paddle. So, the kayaks were placed in the water and we were shown the proper technique (and the not so proper techniques) for paddling, and how to paddle with a partner. That was always a challenge. The person in the stern had to follow the rhythm of the person in the bow. And if you were unlucky enough to have someone who was always distracted and not following a set rhythm as your partner, god help you. Vernon, of course, was yodeling. I loved the feel of the kayak sliding through the salt water, especially when my partner and I were in sync. And I was very glad I had been doing my pushups. I could see how paddling for eight hours a day was going to wear on my arms.

We ventured out to Lion Island and beyond, eventually ending up at a kittiwake rookery. Kittiwakes are members of the gull family who nest on steep rocky cliffs, and the juveniles take three years to mature! This particular rookery was nestled between two waterfalls and there were thousands of birds sitting in pairs on the tiny ledges on the cliff face. Kittiwake pairs had an interesting ritual to recognize their mate. When one bird would return to the nest, they would greet each other and move their heads and necks as though they were regurgitating, then they would rub their necks together. I guess it might be easy to land on the wrong ledge with so many birds in one place! It was a marvelous site to see.

We headed back to Whittier after our visit to the rookery and a beautiful first paddle. Once on shore, the last item of business was to pack up the day bags. Each of us received a big yellow waterproof bag which was chock full of lunch food and snacks, including various types of granola bars and an assortment of candy bars. The Alaska Candy Exchange was on.

Everyone dumped the contents of their yellow bags on the ground and began sorting out what they liked and what they didn't. There were piles of Snickers here, cinnamon and apple granola bars there. Mountains of candy bars began to rise from the gravel-covered ground. The excitement was hard to contain and soon the spirited trading began.

"I'll trade you my Snickers for a Baby Ruth!" I shouted.

"Here's two Clark bars for a Mars bar!" someone else yelled.

It was sheer chaos as our animated group in head nets were dickering and dealing, and candy bars flew through the air from one side of the group to the other as deals were sealed. Even the granola bars were not immune to the swap as they, too, flew by. Passerby's began to gather and watch what appeared to be the New York Stock Exchange occurring right there in Whittier. Tourists asked to pose with us for pictures. In the end, most everyone was happy with their bounty and the yellow day bags were repacked with our edible treasures. With that we were ready to embark on our wilderness adventure.

Now the challenge would be how to ration my treats. Twenty-five days with a bag full of chocolate was going to be a very long time.

Journey to Base Camp

There are many things to think about when you are kayaking in the ocean, especially in Alaska. The water is cold, so cold that if you were to capsize your life would end in minutes. There are large chunks of ice that break off from the glaciers and float around in the water, and they can easily puncture a fragile kayak. These beautiful blue glaciers melt into milky streams that flow into the bays, keeping the water frigid. The summer weather in Prince William Sound went from comfortably warm to cold enough to lay frost on the tents, all within a few weeks. And it was rainy. Either a constant mist or actual rainfall.

Cold and dampness were major concerns due to hypothermia, and if you couldn't take care of your medical emergency in the field, you were in trouble. So, safety was always in the forefront of our minds.

There were two main activities that required organization, paddling and meal preparation. We were assigned a different kayak partner each day so that if by chance you shared a boat with someone whose paddling style did not match yours, you could be assured of having a new partner the next day. Evening meals were prepared by two individuals (with no menus!) and so two people would be assigned as cooking partners every day. They would be responsible for feeding the entire camp. I never had the same partner for cooking and paddling in the same day.

We left Whittier to begin our journey to base camp which was located some two hundred miles east in Icy Fjord on July 27, 1985. For safety and comfort's sake, we hugged the shoreline rather than go out into open water and paddled through the Passage Canal. What a sight we must have been. Nine yellow kayaks and one forest green, our white paddles dipping in one side then the other pulling the boats through the cold seawater. We moved like a flock of ducks, coming together and going apart. Some sang songs. Others just watched the splendor. Vernon yodeled and told stories.

I was crammed into my kayak like a sardine. Gear surrounded me, my camera bag and yellow day bag were shoved between my legs. I could hardly move. The cockpit was covered by a kayak skirt which protected everything from getting wet. I wore my Helly Hansen bibs and raincoat made of thick PVC over the top of several layers of shirts. Fleece pants and long underwear kept my legs warm, and thick wool socks with liners and knee-high rubber boots protected my feet. I wore gray wool gloves and a hat that that kept my hands and head warm. Keeping warm and staying dry were critical. We had no issues with blackflies while we were paddling on the water. But if we were going to pull onto shore for a break, the head nets came back out but quick.

When it was time for our mid-morning snack and pee break, we had to look for a beach that had plenty of room to pull up the kayaks. This was not always an easy find, because the coastline was very rocky. But eventually there would be a nice pull off spot and we would line up the kayaks side by side and untangle ourselves from the gear which held us in. Out came the yellow day bags. After a short mid- morning break we would then head back out to the water and continue on our journey. Lunch and midafternoon break looked the same as the midmornings, with the exception of a few games of hacky sack and a nap or two. After a few days, it was clear that the sooner you emptied your day pack the lighter your kayak would be, so everyone wanted to offer lunch items from their day bag first.

Remember when I said that kayaking would be a piece of cake for me since I am a canoeist? Well, I wasn't sure how I felt about kayaking those first few days. It was hard to get the feel of the boat and it was very slow going, I was used to canoeing on rivers and lakes. And even though I had done my pushups, my arms and back muscles were sore! In fact, I developed tendonitis in my forearm muscle so bad I had a huge knot and had to get a new paddling partner!

As the afternoons wore on, we would start looking for places to camp for the night. When we found a potential site, we first had to find the high tide line to make sure our tents wouldn't be washed away during the night. This line was usually indicated by a

156

row of washed up vegetation higher up on the beach. Our professor, Suzanne Marcy, would consult the high tide table to find out when we could expect the water level to rise, and, if everything was satisfactory, we set up camp. After a while we all became proficient at reading the tables.

Using the facilities required a bit of planning. Because we carried all our gear, everything was rationed including toilet paper. Suzanne, gave us instructions on proper toilet etiquette. Each of us had enough toilet paper to last us for our trip, meaning one roll. We were only to use three squares for each potty break. The used toilet paper was then to be put into a Ziploc bag to be burned at the evening "burning the toilet paper" ritual. "Eeewww yuck!" could be heard coming from the mouths of most of us. "Trust me, you do not want to run out of toilet paper. Three squares only!" Suzanne said. We were to defecate in the intertidal zone, she told us, so that our waste would be carried out to sea during low tide. This was especially important when we were in base camp, as we stayed in the same place for nine days. More comments came forth, none fit to print.

At the campfire on our first night out in the bush, Suzanne said "It's time!" and pulled out her baggie of used toilet paper. "No!" screamed the rest of us. Can you imagine how humiliating it would be to burn used toilet paper in front of everyone? "We'll do this all together," she said, trying to encourage us. Suzanne whipped out her bag of toilet paper, unzipped it, and pulled out the once white tissue. "Agh!" yelled the crowd. With a flamboyant swoosh, she tossed it into the flames and in an instant, it was gone. "Who's next?" she asked.

One night about two o'clock in the morning we heard yelling. Everyone unzipped their tents and jumped out into the darkness trying to see where the commotion was originating. Oh, please don't let it be a bear, I thought to myself. It wasn't long before we saw a tent being licked by the rising tide and two guys pulling out their sleeping bags and clothes, tossing them further up onto the shore. "Help us!" they cried, so we all jumped in and rescued the tent from the icy grip of the ocean. Apparently, they had set it up a tad too close to the high tide line and as a result awoke to a very wet surprise. Luckily their gear and bags were not soaked, but the tent was another matter. It was hung up in a tree to dry, and they each found another tent to take them in for the night. We just shook our heads and went back to bed.

We averaged about fifteen miles per day on our journey to base camp. Our daily routine remained pretty much the same. Wake up, pack up, eat, paddle, break for snack, break for lunch, break for snack, set up camp. Sometimes we took exploratory side trips such as the day we went to a salmon stream on Culross Island where the salmon were so thick they actually bumped our kayaks when we paddled through.

When we got to Tigertail Glacier, a beautiful blue hunk of ice we could see off in the distance, Suzanne asked if we wanted to cross open water and go see it. She warned us the open water would be more difficult to paddle through as it was choppy compared to near shore. But we all wanted to see this glacier up close and personal, so we started paddling toward it. We paddled for nearly a half hour and didn't seem to get one-foot closer to the glacier.

"What's going on?" I asked. "Why aren't we getting any nearer?" I was becoming quite tired by then. Suzanne laughed and said, "That glacier is miles and miles away, it is so big that it appears you can paddle right up to it, but actually it would take us a very long time to get there!"

I have to admit that was a great teaching moment. We spent a few minutes floating in Prince William Sound admiring the beauty that surrounded us then slowly turned the kayaks around and headed back to the calmer water of the shoreline to continue our journey to Tigertail camp.

Harbor Seals and Floating Ice

In western science, one way to study the behavior of an animal is to develop an ethogram, an inventory of behaviors. That way we have an accurate assessment of what an animal is doing at any given point in time, without human interpretation of intent. And that was the method we used in Prince William Sound to study the behavior of harbor seals.

Our base camp was set up on the opposite side of a ridge from Icy Fjord about two hundred miles east of Whittier, Alaska. A narrow trail led up the to the top of that ridge then down the other side to an open area perfect for observing the hundreds of harbor seals that were perched on the ice chunks floating in the bay below. We took that trail on the first day of the study and had an introduction to just how we would be collecting data on the marine mammals. As we crossed the ridge, a mother willow ptarmigan feigned injury and fluttered off in one direction while her babies scampered into the bush in the opposite direction. We made sure to be noisy as there were many bears in the area due to spawning salmon in the nearby streams.

Once we reached the opening, we all sat down on the cold ground and took out our binoculars and spotting scopes. As far as we could see there were harbor seals and ice floats. Our professor showed us the boundaries of our study area, projections of land framing the fjord. We scanned the ice looking closely at what the seals were doing.

We were assigned a research partner and each pair would take a two-hour shift sometime during the study period which began at six in the morning and ended at dusk. We were to look at each seal and then call out a number that corresponded to the behavior it was exhibiting the moment we saw it. That way, not only did we collect behavioral information, we also counted how many seals there were. For instance, the number one meant *prone*, two *head or flippers up*, and three *head movement lateral or otherwise*. We started the study the next day, bright and early. The unlucky pair who drew first shift grumbled up the ridge to the observation post, took out their binoculars and notebooks, and began to search water for seals. "Six, two, two, one, six, two," said the observer. The other person recorded the numbers. The count was done every half hour until they were relieved by the next crew. And on and on it went until supper time. One observer noted blood on the ice and after careful inspection with the binoculars determined that the seal laying on it had been shot. The mammal was still alive but we couldn't tell how severe its wound was. That was sad to see. Apparently, fishermen were not fond of seals because they believed the seals stole fish from their nets and would often shoot at them.

At the end of the day, the last pair of observers would trudge into camp and we would eat our supper together, have a lecture on Darwin's theory of evolution, and end the day with a beautiful campfire to send us to sleep. It was like being in another world. Rather, heaven.

Wet Socks and Butterfingers

July and August are fairly rainy months in Prince William Sound. On those rare sunny days, everyone would pull out their dirty clothes and wash them in the ice-cold streams. Then they would be hung out to dry over makeshift clotheslines, and we would hope that all the moisture would be gone by the time the sun went down. Because sure as Shinola it would rain the next day. Guaranteed.

If by chance your clothes didn't get dry enough during the day, you could stuff them into the bottom of your sleeping bag and by morning your body heat will have finished the job. This was especially useful for wool socks, which always seemed to be wet. It was also common to put the next day's clothes in the sleeping bag with you as well, so they would be toasty warm the next morning when you had to put them on.

Toward the end of the trip, we had a very wet day and my clothes got quite damp. I became cold and just couldn't get warm. So, that night, I put those damp clothes in my sleeping bag with me and didn't sleep a wink as I was shivering all night. In the morning, not only were the clothes still wet but my sleeping bag was, too. And I was chilled to the bone. A wet bag is deadly in the bush, if you have no chance to dry it.

We spent the day paddling in a fine mist and I was still very cold and damp. We eventually stopped at an island and it wasn't long before I started to become a bit delirious. I was becoming hypothermic and needed to get warmed up fast. One of my female friends offered to be my bag buddy and we both got into and under a bunch of dry sleeping bags, her naked body pressed against mine for warmth. "Do you need anything else?" someone asked. "Yes, yes. I need chocolate," I weakly whispered, "Butterfingers." It wasn't long before I had a pile of Butterfinger candy bars under the covers with me. It seemed like it took several hours before I finally warmed up. But that was the last time I put wet clothes in my sleeping bag at night.

Salt Water Daiquiri

We had been working very hard on our study of harbor seals and our personal research projects and it was a beautiful day, so our professor graciously gave us a holiday to go on an adventure. We could choose between visiting a puffin rookery or paddle to an island that was supposed to have lots of sea otters living around it. Oh, how I wanted to see puffins! But because I was studying sea otter feeding behavior, I opted to go to the island.

We loaded up our day bags, jumped into the kayaks, and headed off for a much-needed day of discovery! After several hours of paddling through fairly calm waters we finally made it to the island, only to find that there were hardly any sea otters around! You can imagine how disappointed I was, given how much I had wanted to see the puffins. But we still had a great time exploring the island.

We began our paddle back to base camp in the late afternoon. All of a sudden as we got close to the mountain range that guarded our camp, we were paddling through what appeared to be a giant salt water daiquiri! We had neglected to check the tide tables when we left and were now returning during low tide, which had carried out all the slush from the calving glaciers! The setting sun sparkled against the sea of crushed ice with the mountains draped behind, and it was one of the most beautiful sites I had ever seen. Our professor was very concerned, however, as the ice could puncture a kayak easily and if we took on water and capsized, our chance of survival would have been next to nothing. So, we were instructed to paddle carefully and quickly back to camp.

On that particular trip, I was in the stern and had been taking a number of photographs all day. And as luck would have it, a harbor seal decided to swim right next to our kayak as we moved through the salt water daiquiri. Of course, I couldn't let that opportunity pass by, so for most of the time I had my paddle laying across the cockpit and was snapping pictures of the seal and the beautiful, sparkling scenery around me. My paddling partner was none too happy with me and yelled at me several times to paddle. But I couldn't help myself, I wasn't going to miss the opportunity of a lifetime to get some great shots of paddling through a salt water daiquiri.

At last we broke through the slushy ice and had calm waters back to camp. My paddling partner didn't speak to me the rest of the night, but I was happy. I had just taken some of the most beautiful photographs of the trip. And no one capsized.

Death by Black Fly

"Barbara Jean Barton, 27, of Three Rivers, Michigan, passed away suddenly in Prince William Sound, Alaska. Ms. Barton was in the wilderness studying marine mammals when she choked on a black fly..."

This was the vision in my mind as I stood gasping for breath in Prince William Sound, Alaska.

We had stopped at an incredible island that was most definitely a rainforest, every plant seemed larger than life and I expected a giant brontosaurus to appear at any minute. Along one path was a blanket of brilliant green moss draped over a smooth boulder, flowing as though it thought itself an ocean wave. There were ferns over four feet tall, plants I didn't know whose leaves were as big as my torso. It was spectacular.

As we were walking along exploring this beautiful place, I inhaled a black fly through my mouth. Black flies are tiny little beasts that bite like the dickens. During most of our trip we wore head nets to protect ourselves against them, but for some reason on that lunch break I didn't have mine on. This little black fly lodged itself somewhere down my throat in such a way that everything required to cough or breathe was paralyzed. I stood there choking, but not really choking, for that was frozen, too. I grabbed my throat and began to realize that I might choke to death. It was in that moment the obituary ran through my mind. No, I couldn't have died being mauled by a grizzly, or ripped to shreds by one of the killer whales we saw, I had to die from inhaling a black fly.

One of the co-leaders of the trip happened to glance my way and noticed I was turning a beautiful shade of blue. She quickly ran over and was ready to administer the Heimlich maneuver when I vomited up the little black fly. I gasped for air and dropped to my knees, eyes watering and heart pounding. And then I started to laugh. And laugh. And laugh.

I thanked my lucky stars that day that I didn't have to leave this

164

world known as the girl who died by black fly. I wore my ugly green head net every time I was on land from that day forward.

Missing Backpacker

Prince William Sound is one of the most beautiful places I have been to. There are glaciers and mountains rimming ice cold bays and fjords, and a sky filled with billions of stars. My month-long research trip studying seals and sea otters was ending, but I just wasn't ready to say goodbye to Alaska. So, I decided to stay an extra week or so with Carmen, one of the co-leaders of the trip.

Our group of sixteen was picked up on Applegate Island by a large boat and we loaded half of the two-person ocean kayaks onto the deck and towed the rest behind us. We road in the boat for several hours, watching the beautiful shoreline whiz by, realizing that this place would soon become a cherished memory. There were sad raccoon faces all around, as sunglasses had made circles within otherwise bronzed skin. Even though it had rained nearly every day we were out, we still tanned and my hair was the blondest it had ever been. In fact, you could almost call it white.

We made our way back to where we began our adventure, the port town of Whittier. From there we took the train and traveled the rails inland along Turnagain Arm to Anchorage, then hopped in some taxis to go get dinner. Our senses had changed so much being out in the bush that the lights and sounds were literally overwhelming. The slightest "ping" from a fork hitting a plate was deafening. Flashing stop lights were blinding. The noise of traffic was overpowering. I was astounded at how desensitized we had become to all this noise pollution. Even using the bathroom was odd, as our toilet for the past month had been the intertidal zone of the ocean, where we could watch starfish, jelly fish, and shrimp entertain us. A living episode of the Undersea World of Jacques Cousteau! Using a porcelain bowl seemed, well, just wrong. Unnatural. We opted to go outside and find some bushes. Now that was better.

Carmen, myself, and another member of our team went to her apartment where we planned to rest a few days, then go out again for more adventures. Carmen's roommate Joe was a ranger for the U.S. Forest Service. As soon as we walked in the door he informed us that there was a missing backpacker in Denali National Park, a young twenty-year-old woman named Jenny who had gone out on a solo trip but had not returned. She was scheduled to meet friends at a train station back home and her friends became worried when Jenny did not show up. They called her family, who then contacted officials. The Park Service rangers needed assistance in the search and put the Alaska Mountain Rescue Group (AMRG) on alert. Carmen and Joe were members.

Carmen looked at me and said, "Well, do you want to join us on the search and rescue mission?"

"Of course," I responded. I was in my twenties then and thought this would be a cool experience to have. "Let's go!"

We were to check in with the rangers at noon on that Sunday at headquarters. We anxiously packed up our gear and arrived at Denali the day before and made camp at Riley Creek, then met up with the search team leader the next day at the agreed upon time. He told us the AMRG had been called up and we were to meet for a briefing early the next morning then take a helicopter out to Jenny's last known location.

Early the next morning, we had one more meeting then were flown out by helicopter to a base camp deep in the park near the area where Jenny's belongings were found. I had never flown in a helicopter before. We rode in a Bell - the one that look like a dragonfly with a glass bubble on the front. We could see everything beneath us. We flew up over a mountain and then the mountain dropped out of sight below, taking my stomach with it. I almost threw up.

After we landed at base camp, our team set up the tents and cooked some food and steamy hot drinks over the roaring one burner backpacking stoves. After filling our bellies, we met with the rest of the team and were briefed on the status of the mission.

The team leader described Jenny's clothing. She was wearing a tan sweater, lavender chamois shirt, and black pants. Her father had been at headquarters since Friday night, and said he and his daughter used to go hiking a lot in the Sierras, where he taught her to always follow the river downstream if she ever got lost. This helped us with our search efforts.

A couple days before we arrived, four rangers had already hiked up Primrose Ridge (her destination) to search for her. Helicopters had been called in and one of the pilots spotted the woman's backpack next to the Sanctuary River. Rescue teams with search dogs were then called out and picked up her scent on both sides of the river, indicating she had lost her pack while crossing it and had made her way out of the water. They speculated she took a route toward the park's only road through a canyon, or perhaps tried to climb the cliffs of Primrose Ridge. Sunday began the search of the river and some of the ridges. The helicopters flew close to the water looking for her body.

It was during the briefing that the reality, the tragedy of the situation sunk into me. This wasn't a cool experience. This was someone's daughter missing, a fellow backpacker. Someone who may be out there injured, crying, alone, or worse. I felt shame, sadness, and determination to find her. I grew up.

Our team was split into two smaller groups where we received instructions. Our group would conduct a line search in the highest priority areas. We were to trek along the west side of the river then head south to the Canyon and east to the edge of the hills. Thirteen of us, four from the AMRG and the rest rangers and park service employees, spread ourselves out in a line an arm's length apart. When the leader yelled "go" we were to walk forward in a straight line through everything. Bushes, rivers, brush, it didn't matter…we were not to deviate from our line. This was to insure we didn't miss a thing. If we found something, we were to shout "stop" and the entire line would come to an immediate halt. The leader would then come and collect whatever we found and record its location. He would then order "go" and we would resume the search.

Not long after we started, I discovered recent human feces in a trench with toilet paper. It was marked and I photographed the area.

I must admit I was scared when we came upon the Sanctuary River. It wasn't deep but it was fast. And those rocks, they were real slippery. I took the first step and almost fell right into the river. I found a stick to use and carefully made my way across the first barrier of stones, into the river, and up the other side, fighting the current and slippery stones the entire time. There were several close calls as I made my way, nearly falling into the icy cold water.

We moved on and again "stop!" was called by one of the searchers, who had found a tent stake. We walked a few more steps then I spotted some strips of white athletic tape and a nickel in the middle of the line. We proceeded on throughout the rest of the day and when we reached the last line, word came that about five hundred yards up the river a helicopter had spotted the arm of a sweater in the water. The water level of the river had lowered during the day and that was what had allowed the sweater to become visible. Further investigation by some climbers and diver confirmed it to be a woman's body which was lodged under a rock. They were unable to free her for quite some time. Finally, they extracted her, only to have the current carry her away.

About a half hour later, reports came in from the crew that Jenny had once again been located and her body secured. The helicopter pilot, a Vietnam Veteran, landed the helicopter on the side of the mountain. How he did this I will never know, but he did. He extended a cable down to the river's edge where Jenny's body had been placed in a black bag. The divers hooked the bag to the cable and the helicopter slowly lifted up and flew away. The memory of that body bag dangling and swinging in the sky is burned into my memory. "Goodbye Jenny," I whispered. How I wish we would have found her alive.

There was a dark somber cloud hanging over the camp as we packed our gear up and flew back to headquarters. We gathered for the debriefing, where Jenny's last moments were described to us as best as could be told from the evidence at the scene. Jenny had crossed the Sanctuary River but fell during her traverse. She had likely developed hypothermia and shed her pack and many of her clothes due to being disoriented. Jenny tried to climb up Primrose Ridge to get to the Park road on the other side, but apparently slipped and fell back into the Sanctuary River where she died. No one spoke a word. A twenty-year-old woman was dead.

I thought of Jenny's family, somewhere in this beautiful wilderness park, receiving the terrible news of the death of their daughter/sister. I thought of all my backpacking adventures and what might have happened to me. I had gained a deep respect for the power of nature and how small and fragile we are.

Some may criticize Jenny for going out alone into the wilderness. But no one I know who has ever spoken against solo trips has ever experienced them. I honor Jenny. She was brave, courageous, and determined. She climbed a mountain to try to reach help even though she was likely injured and hypothermic. She never gave up. But the Sanctuary River wanted her and what the river wants the river gets.

CHAPTER 7

THE OKEFENOKEE SWAMP

I am not sure when I first heard about the Okefenokee Swamp. But I do recall it sounded like an adventure I didn't want to miss. Most of the Swamp lies within the Okefenokee National Wildlife Refuge and Okefenokee Wilderness area, which straddles the Georgia-Florida line. It is the largest "black water" swamp in North America, covering 438,000 acres. Hummock and islands rise from peat bottom that formed from decaying vegetation thousands of years ago.

The Okefenokee is a naturalist's paradise, with over two hundred species of birds, forty species of mammals, over fifty species of reptiles, and sixty species of amphibians. The waters are home to thirty-four species of fish. Indeed, when one paddles into this wildlife haven, you are welcomed with songs and smells like no other.

I decided to plan a canoe trip in the Okefenokee the year after my kayaking adventure in Alaska. The Okefenokee

National Wildlife Refuge has a series of one-way trails that must be reserved well in advance. It is set up this way to minimize human impacts and give visitors an exceptional experience. You feel like you are all alone in the Refuge because you never see another human. It is a wonderful set up for someone like me who wants to be in the solitude of nature. But apparently a lot of others feel the same way, as I learned trying to get a reservation.

I contacted the park one afternoon to inquire about reserving a trail and was told there were no openings. Apparently, people had to call exactly one year ahead of time and even that became difficult as professional guides and outfitters were actually camping out on the doorsteps of the park offices to reserve trips for their clients. Not to be discouraged, I called every single morning until I was finally able to book a four-day trip. My paddling companion was a woman I met during my trip to Alaska, a fellow Michigander named Mary. I called to tell her the exciting news and we set about planning our next adventure, the Okefenokee Swamp.

A few days before we were to depart, I was watching a National Geographic program on the television with my Grandma. We were eating sundaes, of course. There on the screen was a man swimming in the Okefenokee Swamp, grunting like pig. The water was up to his neck as he slowly moved through the darkness. He shined a spotlight over the surface of the water and occasionally two eyes would shine – alligators! The sound he was making was the mating call. I am not sure if he was brave or stupid. Of course, the first thing I thought of was to remember my flashlight and memorize the grunting sounds. I was going gator shining!

Our trip was a memorable one, full of ibises, alligators, anoles, and beautiful flowers. Of note were the large, hungry mosquitos that forced us into tents by midafternoon. As I do on every adventure, I kept a journal on our trip into the swamp. The entries are snapshots in time, unedited and raw. Some of the stories I have long forgotten, some are as fresh as the day they happened. My only regret is that I cannot brush onto these pages the wonderful scents of the hoorah bush and lily pads, or the sounds of the swamp at night. The following entries will have to do.

Canal Run

Today we began our canoe trip into the Okefenokee Swamp. Bob, the concessioner, gave us a hand launching, and also showed me where some great blue herons were nesting. He said it was only a couple of miles out of the way.

We started out down the canal and immediately saw gators along the edges of the water. Most were smaller – eight feet or so. We paddled part way with an old couple named Isabella and Dick Pierson from Pennsylvania and Florida. They had quite a few stories to tell! We enjoyed the morning paddle, seeing many splendid birds – great blue herons, ibises, egrets, little blue herons, green-backed herons, red-shouldered hawks, red-winged blackbirds, boat-tailed grackles. The herons are incredibly large here – I saw one sitting on top of a snag that appeared to be six feet tall! The nests we saw had young; one had two babies, the other two nests had solo occupants. We watched as an adult fed the two young ones. They were quite loud, as if they hadn't been fed in weeks. The parent jumped down a few feet after feeding the youngsters, and you should have heard them cry!

We paddled through Chesser Prairie and Grand Prairie, before realizing we missed a turn and added about eight miles to our otherwise ten-mile trip. The prairies were great – covered with white pond lilies, golden club, common pipewort, titi, pitcher plants, iris, and pickerelweed. If you didn't see the water, you could almost imagine yourself walking through it. The egrets stood out as they fished in the shallow areas, or stood atop the trees. Alligators called for mates in the distance, grunting like pigs. There were alligator runs all along the edge of the canal, leading into marsh prairies.

One of the neat things I saw in the prairie was what I thought to be a red-shouldered hawk catch a fish. The fish was about eight to ten inches long and was still flopping as the bird proudly flew off.

There are many prothonotary warblers and Swainson's warblers. I've been trying to get a shot of one but have had no luck yet. As I write, a marsh wren flew into the registration box and upon closer inspection, I see it has a nest inside. There are no eggs yet.

We finally turned around and went back to Canal Run. This trail has "banks" lined with cypress and titi and often long leaf pine. There are many gators along this trail — sometimes they surprise you with a big splash, other times they silently sink underwater. Quite mysterious they are — not scary as I thought they would be.

The weather is quite unpredictable. I'm quite severely sunburned. The sun disappeared after lunch and we got drenched. About ten minutes later it was out again. Thunder rolled in the distance. All in all, we did about twenty miles today. The skeeters are trying to carry me off, so I'll sign off for today.

Floyd's Island

Journal entry - April 27, 1988

I have never spent a night like last night! Not long after we went to bed, a raccoon came and tried to get our food. Fortunately, it was tied up good. Not long after, when it was dark, I tried shining for gators. There was one about five feet offshore in front of the tent. It just stayed there and watched me. It was quite exciting. All night there were great sounds of creatures I didn't know. I spent fifteen minutes looking for the source of a cricket-like sound. I have yet to know what it is. All night there were incredible sounds. Time and again I spotted a gator, I was drawn to look by the splashing sound it made when it hunted. If my writing is spotty, it is because I am trying to keep my eyes open for wild animals, as I am laying in the sun on a somewhat beach at the end of a canal. I have been stalked by three raccoons and an anole so far, and I do hear gators in the distance. One could easily grab my legs as I am very close to the water.

Anyhow, I couldn't sleep well because I had to stay awake to hear everything. The last noise was a barred owl that woke up both of us this morning. It was just across the canal and was very loud!

I shined in the water last night and saw a crayfish and some minnows. Of course, you can't see very deep because of the color of the water.

We headed to Floyd's Island under very sunny skies. The humidity was quite low for a change. We passed a few gators in the channel before we entered Chase Prairie. There were many more lily pads in this prairie, plus pitcher plants, golden club, pipewort, and iris. Gators were bellowing all around us. We paddled within two feet of one and didn't even see it! Fortunately, it was friendly and didn't charge us. Ibises were feeding with their sideward head movement on both sides of us. We scared up a great white cloud of them. Many herons again as well as egrets. I have a bad sunburn.

The mosquitoes are quite miserable and prevent any substantial time outdoors. I refuse to use bug dope, so I am covered with bites. I can't see visiting here any later in the season. There are so many insects that you can hear a continuous buzz in the air. They have a particularly large bee-like insect that makes a hell of a lot of noise. You hope it never stings you! They live in wooden structures like the cabin we are in.

The channel to Floyd's Island was quite shallow. We were afraid we would have to portage. My paddle never reached solid ground! There was a dead beaver in the water. I tried to cut off its tail but it was too tough. I thought it strange that the beaver had bite marks all over it but was left in the water like that. [I later learned from the man who picked us up that gators kill their prey then let them rot for a few days before eating them! I could have been gator food!]

We are spending the night in a beautiful hunting cabin. It has three bedrooms, a porch, fireplace, and outhouse. I was quite surprised by the 'niceness' of the structure. Haven't seen much wildlife, except three pesky raccoons — one with a bad hind leg. Going shining later on.

Went out later and didn't see anything. But what a night. We had mice trying to break into our food and then they ran over my head and one flew into my bag! And then! I saw a bug at least a foot long crawl under the door — a giant cockroach! It was carrying an egg case. Mary got the cockroach out, but smashed its eggs. In the middle of the night I felt something bite my leg. I shined my flashlight into the bag and out pops another foot-long cockroach! It tried to get away but I smashed it. We would have had better sleep in a tent! All the night I was crammed into my bag with the drawstring pulled tight so nothing could get into my bag. Gosh did I sweat! Finally, I gave in and unzipped it. I was open game for cockroaches and mice. I think I got twenty minutes sleep all night. When I awoke, the smashed cockroach was gone!

Bluff Lake

Journal entry of April 28, 1988. Sunny, 85-90 degrees

We headed out this a.m. for Bluff Lake, about eight and a half miles. Our travels took us through some beautiful prairie once again. We kicked up many colonies of feeding ibises, egrets, little blue herons. They were splendid as these white birds exploded into the sky. I hope to have captured some on film. My sun burn is a little better on my legs, however, they are still quite swollen. My back is sore, too. Otherwise I am in good shape.

This last run was a killer. One and a half miles of water/peat six inches deep. We could barely pole through some spots, and barely paddle through others. It was quite challenging and I am glad to say we didn't have to get out of the boat and push! If we would have met a gator...I shudder to think of it! I did get to see lovely sundews (a great photo!), pitcher plants and iris.

There was another close paddle to a gator – a huge one! Fortunately, it let us go by. The campsite at Bluff Lake is a wooden platform with a roof over it and a great outhouse. There is a small gator across the channel that has been there for several hours. I guess its sleeping.

I feel a little homesick today, guess I want to share this experience with my loved ones back home. It has been good with Mary – we travel well together.

Night time was dreamlike. The moon was almost full, and the sky clear. Stars sparkled like diamonds. I saw the dipper, but couldn't find Orion. Gators bellowed everywhere around us. There were probably fifty or more. Some called with greater frequency than others. Many frogs were chirping as well as a few birds. There are sandhill cranes behind us that made a very loud vocal display. Then another group to the east answered. It was neat. Barred owls also joined in the chorus. This morning (Friday April 28) we had a beautiful sunrise. I took some great shots of the mist rising up over the canal into the sunrise. I think this is one the nicest places I've ever been. We are perched right in the middle of a prairie.

Traders Hill Campground

Journal entry of April 29, 1988. Sunny, 85-90 degrees

We had a nice paddle today through prairies and several small lakes — Bluff, Half Moon, Durdin, Flag, and Elder. The lakes were small with tall, yellow water lilies on the edge. The sandhills gave us a goodbye cry and two even flew over us. I called to them and they answered. Even the barred owls cried from a distance. We had smooth water up to the three-mile mark, then the wind was against us. We had a tough time paddling, but we did it. We only saw one gator today swimming in a lake. Mary thought she saw a rail. We did see black and turkey vultures. All in all, this was an excellent trip, well worth repeating although our pick-up person suggests the red and green trails. We are going to go on the green trail at Steven Foster tomorrow.

Let me tell you about an old man named Tommy. Tommy works at the Traders Hill Campgrounds and has for seventeen years. He has a funny face; his mouth is somewhat recessed and contorts with every word. He calls me ma'am and honey. Tommy tells me he used to work as a conservation officer back in the 1950s, capturing alligator poachers. According to him, the poachers would have bird meal flown in from Mexico and dropped by plane into the swamp "to feed the alligators." A skin back then was worth five hundred dollars if it was a big one. Well, Tommy found out that there were three reasons he couldn't stay working in the swamp. Deer flies, yellow flies, and horse flies. He is allergic to them and swells up like a balloon when one bites him. So, the government gave him more money and sent him to Traders Hill where he has been ever since. Now, Tommy's wife was born on Billy's Island, a spot he calls one the most beautiful around. There were once two-hundred fifty people on that island, working the lumber. Then the government bought it up and wanted to turn it into a park. All of the residents had to leave and their beautiful cypress homes were burned to the ground. He says today you can go and still see remnants of the civilization.

We will go there tomorrow and find out. I want to talk with Tommy more but he is gone for today and he won't be back until Monday.

After a welcome shower, Mary and I headed to Traders Hill Cemetery. It had some old stones, wooden head stones, and crumbled ones as well. A group of tombs had one family's history all the way back to 1300 A.D. or so. One stone had a letter and pictures of three grandkids taped to the headstone. It was sad. I couldn't believe Mary wanted to pull the letter off and read it. I felt that was very disrespectful! Luckily it wouldn't come off.

Had another interesting talk with the driver of our canoe pick-up. He has been doing pickups for seven or eight years. His dad owns the concessions pad. Well remember the old bloated beaver I found in the channel going to Floyd's Island? The one I tried to cut off the tail but my buck knife "couldn't cut it?" Apparently, gators have an interesting feeding style. We were talking about how aggressive alligators were or were not. He said that during the courtship period the larger males will kill the smaller ones. Now there are a couple of big gators that hang out in the Suwannee Canal by the docks. Every so often, one will carry in another gator or maybe a beaver, and let it float around for a week or so until it becomes "bloated, rotten, and tender." Then it will eat it. "Sometimes," he says, "the smell gets so bad they have to try to take the food away from the gator – not too good for the tourist business, you know." Their method is quite simple – one person draws the gators attention with a long pole, the other person lassos it with a reptile noose. The gator will roll around and around until it ties itself up. Then they can yank the prey out of its mouth. He says the gators will carry around their prey and never leave it.

So back to the beaver...pretty lucky I have an arm left. I guess the gator was out, however when we paddled back through, the beaver was gone. What you learn about wildlife! I should be more careful. That beaver looked like it had been mauled, bite marks on head and gut, intestines and bladder hanging out. I just couldn't figure out why the predator hadn't eaten it. Now I know.

Tommy

I was hoping Tommy would be up early so I could pick his brain for more information. He is sort of "dense" or something, maybe just hard of hearing. I tried to get him to tell me about poaching, he didn't know what the word meant. He did fill me in on a big frog that lives in the swamp. Says its legs are almost a foot long and they taste as good as chicken. All you have to do is "go out with a light at night, take a forked stick to spear em' with, then stick em'. Pliers will do for skinning. Then get them home, flour, salt and pepper, and fry." Tommy says, "They're very tasty, honey."

"Then there is fishing. You go out to the prairie, find a hole about as big around as a wash tub, then throw your line in. Those holes are gator holes and are full of fish." Sometimes gators will be a lying on some firm peat and hang their mouths wide open. Flies and mosquitos are drawn to its tongue and stick to it like flypaper. When the gator gets enough, it goes into the gator cave, opens its mouth, and the fish come to get the bugs. Down comes the jaws and the gator has itself supper!"

CHAPTER 8

ISLE ROYALE

The Jewels of Feldtmann Lake

I have always wanted to find an isolated spot in nature to just sit and be part of that particular day in that particular moment. I wanted to be so still that life would continue on around me without fear of my humanness, now so out of place in the wild. I found such a spot at Feldtmann Lake on the southwestern end of Isle Royale.

The first time I visited this remote Lake Superior Island was as an Artist in Residence back in 1992 when I was selected by the park as a songwriter. I was offered a cozy cabin to stay in and was a grateful guest in the park for three weeks. All that was asked of me was to perform a couple of concerts for the island visitors and, of course, to express my experience of this breathtaking place through songwriting. Indeed, I wrote my most popular song there. "Letter to Joshua" (renamed "My Michigan") was crafted as a letter to my nephew – a heartfelt goodbye to the land that I loved. These were some of the last days in Michigan for me until my return in 2000. I was to do a final concert in Bay Mills in the eastern Upper Peninsula then continue on to my new home in Pennsylvania and job with The Nature Conservancy.

I was an avid backpacker during those years and always wanted to go on a solo trip, but my fear of humans always kept me from going out alone on the trail for an extended period of time. But there I was, on an island isolated from any towns or cities and most humans, so I felt safe. I could think of no better way to experience Isle Royale than take a solo journey across the island. I planned out my route, figuring it would take me six days to get to the Windigo Visitors Center, the location of my final concert. I included a day of rest, that special day I had waited for to sit and be with nature. Feldtman Lake was the last stop before Windigo and sounded like as good a place as any, so it was set.

The trip across the island was spectacular. I did not take a tent with me, only a tarp, and had a great time designing lean-to shelters to sleep under. The shapes and angles totally depended on what anchors were available to me. Sometimes I could tie off to a picnic table, other times I had only rocks and tree branches, but I always stayed dry and protected.

It was ten miles from Siskwit Bay to Feldtmann Lake, and the extreme exhaustion I felt when I arrived was washed away by the profound beauty of the area. I found a small clearing with a view of the lake framed by two spruce trees and set up my camp. My muscles and feet were sore, so I walked out to the water and felt the coolness soothe my toes. I took a short rest on the beach then cooked up my supper and hit the sack. I would begin my solitude the next day.

At some point during the night, I was awakened by the sound of teeth grinding on vegetation and hot expulsions of air wafting over my sleeping face. The fog in my brain lifted quickly and I realized there was a moose feeding on something right next to my head.

I didn't quite know what to do. Female moose can weigh anywhere from four hundred to nearly eight hundred pounds, males nearly twice that. Any way you look at it, one hoof on my

183

precious head and it would be all over.

It was a very still night, so as not to startle the beast, I gently whispered in the most hypnotic way possible "Moose, moose, I'm right here." Silence. "I'm right here," I said again, just in case Bullwinkle's cousin didn't hear me. I heard a shuffle or two and then the moose slowly wandered off into the bushes. My heart was pounding. I questioned my wisdom in using a lean-to as shelter and decided to place a lit tea candle a few feet away from my body so that any future browsers would see me and avoid stepping on my head or any other body part. It took me awhile to get back to sleep.

The sun rose the next morning as it always does and my head still retained its form. After a warm bowl of oatmeal, I grabbed my water bottle, some snacks, my camera, and journal and walked to the water. A well-travelled shoreline all around the lake provided a clear route for the many moose that favored the area for feeding. I thought that if I sat at the edge of the shrubs along the beach, I might have a great view of some moose. So, I smoothed out a spot on the ground, sat down, and got comfortable as I would remain in the same spot for the entire day. Then I waited.

What was to ensue now feels like a dream. Directly behind me in a little shrub was a bird's nest with little baby birds in it, so all day long the parents were flying in and out with morsels of food, literally next to my head. I could hear their little peeps and even the sounds of the parents hopping from one side of the nest to the other. At one point, I watched a dragonfly nymph climb up out of the lake bottom and slowly walk from the water's edge to the spot where I was sitting. It climbed right up my pant leg onto my knee. Of course, the next thing that would have to happen is the nymph would molt and turn into a dragonfly and zoom away. But I didn't know how long that process would take. An hour? A couple of hours? A day? While I wanted to wait and see what happened, I decided it would have been safer for the nymph to continue its development on a sturdy piece of vegetation. I carefully plucked it from my knee and placed it on a nearby stem, where I hope it eventually left on the wing.

I decided to stretch my legs a bit so I stood up, moved around, and walked out into the water. Out of the corner of my eyes something glimmered. I searched and searched, moving around to get different angles and finally caught the sunlight glint off of something lying on the bottom of the lake. I reached down and pulled out a beautiful quartz crystal, half encased in a coral colored sheath like nothing I had ever seen before. What a gift, I thought. I stuck it in my pocket and peered into the water again. More sparkles. When the sun hit the water just right, little diamonds would appear to be scattered all over the bottom, then just as quickly disappear when a cloud would float by. I marveled at the beauty of these crystals and found one that was as large as an acorn. My first thought was to take it home with me, but then I started to feel uncomfortable. This piece of quartz had been there forever, Feldtmann Lake was its home. So, I kissed it and tossed it back into the welcoming water, promising I would come back some day and find it again.

The Torpedo Loon of Feldtmann Lake

It was late afternoon and I had been sitting in my solitude spot since early morning when a loon swam close by. I lifted my binoculars and focused on the feathered icon of the north as it paddled around, periodically diving for food. Sometimes he would dive and I would count the seconds he was submerged, then try to guess where he would pop up. This went on for a while until he decided to rest, floating around on the smooth, glassy surface of the calm water.

I was mesmerized by the striking beauty of this bird as I gazed at him through the glasses. My eyes floated with him, my Spirit resting with his body, and I almost went into a trance. It was in that very moment that BAM! A torpedo shot up out of the water right next to the loon and scared the hell out of him and me. I think we both jumped ten feet into the air as the torpedo went airborne then landed back in the water right next to him. It was another loon! The attacker had snuck up on the object of my gaze under the water and undetected, then exploded to the surface to scare him out of the territory. They went back and forth doing threatening displays for some time before the loser swam away.

One poor loon lost his territory. I lost two years off my life.

CHAPTER 9

FORT INDIANTOWN GAP

The Black Widow and the Regal

Fort Indiantown Gap Military Reservation is a National Guard training center nestled in central Pennsylvania. It blankets Blue Mountain, which is part of the Ridge-and-Valley Appalachian Mountains, and drapes out into the valleys east of the mountain. It has been used as a training ground for U.S. troops since 1933. The land here is battered in some places and pristine in others, with spring-fed streams, dense mountainside woods, timber rattlesnakes, and a rare and beautiful butterfly called the regal fritillary.

I was once a zoologist with The Nature Conservancy and was blessed to have spent several years learning about this magnificent creature. Five summers, in temperatures sometimes over one hundred degrees, were devoted to sprinting through fields, tripping over hidden tank ruts, and dodging troops playing war games. All done with the goal of catching as many butterflies as possible and carefully writing a number on their wings so we could estimate how many there were and how far they flew.

I had been chasing and marking regals all morning, and as I made my way down a dusty tank trail, I noticed something flapping about in a clump of tall grass. Upon closer inspection, the cause of the struggle became obvious – it was a male regal fritillary butterfly caught in a spider web unfamiliar to me. The fine strands seemed to be placed haphazardly between the blades of grass, creating a complex maze of silk. As he continued to struggle to free the one wing that was stuck to the web, out from the deep, dark depths of the grass emerged a large female black widow spider. Spider paused and waited. When Regal tired and could no longer flap his wings, Spider moved in and attached the tip of a second wing to her web, then calmly retreated back into the grass.

For the next half hour, Regal gallantly attempted to free himself. But after about fifteen minutes, his movements would cease and out Spider would come, attaching another wing to her delicate web. When at last all four wings were secured and he could no longer move, Spider delivered a paralyzing bite to the underside of his body. She then, quite literally, rolled him up into a cigar-shaped bundle, starting at the tip of his wing. Once he was neatly packaged, she carried Regal down into the darkness of the grass. I returned to her web daily for the next week but never saw Spider or Regal again. The web? It vanished, too.

It was an odd feeling, watching this drama of nature unfold. Here was a butterfly so rare it was being considered for listing as an endangered species. Here was a butterfly that I had held in my hand only weeks earlier. Yet the black widow spider didn't care - she was hungry. Through this small window, Nature doesn't recognize rarity – a meal is a meal, plain and simple. But in the grand scheme of things, rarity causes shifts in our world, some we can see and some we can't. Shifts in the food chain. Shifts in processes. Shifts in quality of life. What will our world be like without the polar bears and seals when the ice caps are gone? What did we lose when the passenger pigeons no longer graced the skies? I watch the clouds of red-winged blackbirds in the fall and can only imagine. There is an Indigenous teaching that says what we do the Earth we do to ourselves. Something to think about.

C4 and Lemons

Line transects are an ecological field technique one might use to look at plant cover. You basically stake out a line of string, say 25 meters long. Then, starting at one end or the other, you stand directly over the string and slowly move forward, measuring the distance any given plant grows directly under the string. So, you might end up with 4.2 cm of grass, 2.7 cm bare soil, and so on. It is a long and tedious process.

One hot afternoon my field assistant Brandon and I were conducting line transects on Range D3, which was best described as a battered old field bisected by tank trails. Paralleling the base of nearby Blue Mountain was a long, linear berm with a hidden tracked target behind it that would appear and disappear during tank firing exercises. And, like everywhere else on the base, the ground was littered with spent shell casings, flare shells, and small silk parachutes. That day, however, we found something new.

Scattered over the field were fragments of plastic lemons. I am sure you know them, the realistic looking plastic citrus you buy in the grocery store that are filled with concentrated lemon juice? Bits of yellow plastic dotted the field like small summer flowers. Most were melted and clearly were the remains of some type of explosion. As we walked around the field, I discovered a golf-ball size chunk of C4, a plastic explosive compound, lying in the dirt. I picked it up, stuck it in my pocket, and continued patrolling my study site. There, in the middle of the field, was a whole, plastic lemon. An unexploded, handmade, lemon grenade. Hmm. Interesting.

As I did every time I found an unexploded something, I got out my bag phone and called it in to Range Control. I left the lemon grenade, walked five meters over to my line transect, and began the long process of counting plant cover. Brandon recorded the data.

I was about half way through when Range Control and the EOD (Explosive Ordnance Disposal) trucks appeared. Out jumped several uniformed military personnel. "Good morning, Ma'am," greeted the Range Control Sergeant. "Morning, Sarge." I replied, feet firmly planted on either side of my transect line. "This here's the Butterfly Lady," Sarge said to the bomb squad guy. In the five years I worked there, they never knew my name. I was simply the Butterfly Lady. "Nice to meet ya," I said. I told them what we had found that morning and handed the bomb squad guy the C4 I had been carrying in my pocket. "S#*t!" he said, rather loudly. I then pointed to the lemon grenade not fifteen feet away.

The bomb squad guy went back to his truck and put on his giant protective suit, the kind you see them wear on the news during a bomb scare somewhere. Feet still firmly planted over the staked-out string that marked my line transect, I watched as he made his way back to the lemon grenade. He looked it over from a distance then slowly walked up to me.

"Ma'am, I am going to have to ask you to go back behind those vehicles for your own safety. We don't know how stable the lemon is."

"I can't go back behind those vehicles right now, I am in the middle of a line transect young man. The middle! I have to finish this transect first," I stated as firmly as the two planted feet pressed into the dry ground that had not moved an inch since his arrival.

"Well Ma'am, then I am going to have to position myself between you and that ordnance until you are done," he proclaimed. Wow, he was willing to risk his life for me to finish my line transect. I said thank you and continued my work, he placed himself directly between me and that little yellow lemon.

Several more vehicles arrived in the fifteen minutes it took for me to finish up my transect. Men with jackets that had big bold letters across their backs that read "FBI" and "ATF". Uh oh.

I no longer argued when ordered into the back seat of the sedan. Question after question about where we had been the day before, the day before that, the night before, what are we doing now, what was I doing with C4 in my pocket? How did I feel about lemons? Were the men going to wear me down, force me into a confession with their barrage of questions, confusing me? Do I like lemons or don't I? What time did I really get up that morning?

There I was, an endangered species biologist studying a very rare butterfly on a military base, with soldiers who loved to drive tanks, bomb, and strafe the butterfly's habitat. Of course, I would be a likely suspect. I am sure images of the crazy Butterfly Lady in her kitchen whipping up Real Lemon hand grenades filled with C4 danced in their heads. We were, after all, dressed in fatigues. We did look like ecoterrorists, well, except for the butterfly nets.

Protocol dictates the EOD must blow up all unexploded ordnances, so charges were set. We all ducked behind the vehicles and covered our ears. "Fire in the hole, fire in the hole, fire in the hole!" the bomb guy yelled. Then, KABOOM! The lemon grenade was no more. In its place was a crater, the kind you see on the moon. I panicked for a second, but then was flooded with relief. My line transect was undisturbed.

After the FBI, the ATF, the MPs, EOD, and Range Control were convinced we didn't make the lemon grenades, they jumped back in their vehicles and sped off down the road.

I decided not to mention the unexploded ordnance we found on the tank trail. We just left that for another day.

Huey Helicopters

Every generation has their war. Mine was Vietnam. I grew up with the nightly news images of flag draped coffins exiting cargo planes, napalm fire storms washing across the jungle, protests and arrests. The heartbreak and confusion, the sorrow and the loss. I have known Vietnam veterans, some who have talked about it and some who just want to forget. I have a Vietnamese friend whose family got out of Saigon on the very last airlift, her uncle forging papers to get them to freedom. She was just a baby then and never spoke much about it other than to say they live in the refuge camps in Thailand for a time before coming to America.

Helicopters are a great way to survey habitat. When I first stepped into a Huey, I immediately wondered if it had been in the war, clear across the ocean in a land I have never seen. Of course, it had. I imagined it carrying troops or wounded soldiers in and out of the jungle. I searched the walls for holes, the floor for blood.

I probably flew in Hueys four or five times. Each pilot was different. One pilot decided to show me how a helicopter would patrol the mountains in time of war. We crept along the ridge, just out of sight, and would pop up occasionally to see what was going on over the ridge. We would zigzag and dart, up and down and around the valley and mountains. I always got sick. "Land, land," I would try to say into the little microphone, fearing I would lose it right then and there. We would find a clearing and I would take a walk to relieve the churning in my gut. "It is all in your head, you know", the pilot told me. "Your body isn't really sick, your mind makes you think you are." "Right," I said, between barfs.

"They are going to retire the Hueys," one pilot told me, sadly. I felt sad, too. I don't know why. Those army green choppers hold a place in my heart, a chord that attaches me to a little white house in Westerville, Ohio when my parents were still together. They remind me of a time when our nation was confused and at war with itself. I was just a child, but I knew.

192

Feeding Spider

Orb weavers are a group of spiders that spin the familiar spider webs we all know and love. Their webs are designed to capture prey, which the spiders immobilize and save for a rainy day. Here then is the tale of Feeding Spider.

There was a low-lying area where I used to survey for butterflies. It was mostly filled with grasses and joe-pye-weed, and in late summer this field was splashed with the deep purple of ironweed flowers. And it was home to a whole village of spiders.

Most every visit I made to this spot was in the early morning hours. The dew would settle on the tall vegetation and soak my pants clean through. Tiny droplets of water would hang from spider webs strung between blades of grass.

One particular morning I made my way into the field, and I noticed that most of the webs had small bundles attached to them. Upon closer inspection, I saw these bundles were grasshoppers and other unfortunate insects that had gotten tangled up in the webs and were subsequently wrapped in spider silk into neat, tidy bundles.

It took much agility on my part to wind my way through the field and avoid all those spider webs. I had watched a spider once construct a web from start to finish. I knew how much work it took. I was not going to destroy one web that day.

As I made my way through the wet vegetation, I saw that I had indeed walked through a web, and one of those wrapped bundles had stuck to my fatigues. I didn't want to waste this tender morsel, so I carefully took a small stick and placed the bundle on the tip.

After a bit of searching, I found what I was looking for. A spider with an empty web. She was hunkered down at its edge, waiting for some action. I don't think Spider was expecting me.

I know that birds and squirrels and cats and dogs all take food from us humans if offered. I wondered if Spider would, too. I took my stick and slowly put the bundle that had stuck on my pants in front of Spider. "Here you go little one," I said. She backed up rather quickly. I remained calm and slowly moved the bundle a little closer. "It's ok Spider, it is a gift from me to you." Slowly Spider moved toward the bundle and very gingerly took my gift. She placed it carefully onto her web, where it stuck like glue.

To Be Taught by a Butterfly

Catching butterflies with a net is an art if you don't want to hurt the delicate beings. The easiest way (easy unless it is a fast flying species in which case you must be extremely quick) is to locate a butterfly that is busy nectaring (feeding) on a flower. You hold the net in your dominant hand and swing gently, not unlike a forehand shot in tennis (remember I said gently). The arch should end on an upstroke, then a quick clockwise circle so as to make the narrow end of the cone-shaped net flip over the rim of the circular frame. This ensures the butterfly cannot fly back out. It is also a move to be done delicately, as the little creature can become trapped between the folds of the net and metal rim, with fatal results.

I spent several summers in the hot Pennsylvania heat chasing and catching regal fritillaries, beautiful orange and iridescent black butterflies similar in size to a monarch. Regals love to nectar on the bright orange butterflyweed and would become so fixated on drinking that you could pluck them right off a flower with your fingers. This work was part of a mark-release-recapture study used to estimate the size of their population and also to document how far they would fly. The methods of this kind of study were simple. I caught the insect, wrote a tiny number on the forewing using an ultrafine point marker, and then let it go with the hope of capturing it later.

One day, I took a civilian employee of the Army out in the field with me to help catch and mark regals. He was in charge of natural resources on the base and was eager to get his feet wet, so to speak. I showed him the proper technique for catching a butterfly and watched as he practiced on invisible insects landing on flowers. When he looked like he had it down, I sent him off on his own. It wasn't long before he shouted, "There's one!" He ran to the flower where the regal was nectaring, wound up, and swung like he was Martina Navratilova. My heart sunk. I quickly took the net and peered inside. Flapping helplessly on the bottom was a female regal fritillary, her right wing completely broken in half.

195

He, of course, felt horrible. In his excitement, he had ended the normal life of a butterfly that was one step below being listed as a federal endangered species. I carefully took the regal out of the net and tenderly placed her in a small cage. If I left her there in the field, she would die a very unpleasant death (at least by my standards). On her remaining wing I saw "7", my lucky number. So, I made the decision to take her home. That was the beginning of our three months together.

Caring for Seven was no easy task. She had to be fed sugar water numerous times every day. She could not fly and perch like her former self, but instead made her way around the square, screened cage by walking. To teach her to drink, I had to carefully hold the edges of her wings between my fingers, then take a pin and insert it in the center of the coil of her proboscis, unwinding the long tongue so that it would touch the syrup. Once the tip hit the water, she drank eagerly.

Over the next few weeks, Seven began to deteriorate. Parts of her wings began to break off. She was living an unnatural life, one much longer than she would have had she been flying free in the fields. But it was during this time that she was the greatest teacher. No matter how difficult her challenges, Seven would persevere. She would still climb up the side of her cage, with little left but stubs where her beautiful wings once were, and sit in the warm sunshine. By this time, I had to physically hold her body while helping her feed. Many times a day. We shared a bond that is hard to describe.

I went on a trip to North Carolina to attend a spiritual retreat, and Seven rode right along with me. We stopped several times throughout the day, me eating my sandwiches and she eating her syrup. At the retreat, many women spent quiet time with her, watching and listening with their hearts. Each one felt moved by the experience. Butterfly is known to be a teacher of rebirth, Seven taught many things, but the most important lesson I received was to never give up, no matter the challenges. Even though Seven had no wings left, she would still attempt to climb her cage walls, seeking the warmth of the sun.

The day George Bush senior was elected president, Seven went to the Spirit world. I placed her tiny body on a square of white silk and sat under the full moonlight with her. This little being had been an intimate part of my life for three months and my heart was saddened by her passing. But as I saw her Spirit rise out of her body with full, gorgeous wings and fly upward into the moon, the sadness in my hearted lifted. Seven was free.

CHAPTER 10

BOG RIVER

The War of the Dragonflies

In the Western Adirondack Mountains in New York, you will find one of the most beautiful paddling trips east of the Great Lakes. The Bog River Flow (Lows Lake) is fourteen and a half miles of scenic, unspoiled beauty with bogs, eagles, and the largest concentration of loons in the state of New York. The campsites are so far apart that you can be there for days and never see another soul. On one trip up the river, I had a very unique experience that even baffled a Clark Shiffer, a colleague and well-respected dragonfly and damselfly expert. I witnessed murder and sabotage in the dragonfly world. Here, then, is the story of the Bog River.

My friend Brenda and I were camping at our favorite site amongst the hemlocks and Canada mayflowers, taking day trips paddling around the large lake, exploring beaver dams and bouncing on the floating bog mats.

I spent several days sitting on the beach, watching the water. I noticed that in mid-afternoon, the dragonflies changed guard. The flying fairies most prevalent in the early afternoon hung out in the shrubs along the shoreline. But precisely at 3:00, they disappeared, and a larger dragonfly species took their place, flying out over the still water. A third type of dragonfly overlapped both shifts, appearing about 2:00 pm and departing the scene around 5:00 pm.

To aid in this story, I must give names to these latter two species to avoid confusion in you, the reader. So, the larger dragonfly I shall refer from here on out as the egg chain dragonfly, and the other the lily pad dragonfly. I do not know their proper names, regrettably.

On one particular afternoon I watched the lily pad dragonfly laying her eggs. She would land on a pad, tip her abdomen into the water up under the lily pad, and deposit them. She would lay several times under one pad, then fly to another and repeat the process again. Every once in a while, a bass would jump up and snatch a lily pad dragonfly, then disappear down into the tea-colored water happy and fat.

The egg chain dragonfly had a completely different strategy for laying her eggs. She would make arched flights downward and release a gel-covered chain of eggs into the water. If you have ever seen a hummingbird doing its U-shaped dive flight, that is what the egg chain dragonfly looks like as she delivers the next generation of dragonflies to the world.

Here is the fantastic part. So, I am watching the lily pad dragonfly doing her thing, when all of a sudden, the egg chain female swoops down and lays a gooey sticky strand of eggs precisely over the body and wings of the lily pad female. Up she flew and began her dive like Snoopy fighting the Red Baron, laying another strand on top of the now helpless lily pad female. Three strands of eggs later, the lily pad dragonfly was done in, completely engulfed in gel. The bass didn't miss a beat and jumped up for dessert. Survival of the fittest.

But it didn't end there. This female continued to seek out lily pad dragonflies and dive bomb them with egg chains, essentially sticking them to the top of the lily pad and preventing any further egg laying by the helpless females. I had never seen anything like this before or since. My friend Clark had also never witnessed anything so bizarre in his forty plus years of watching these beautiful insects. I felt blessed to see such wonder in nature.

It is amazing to think about all of the encounters that go on in our natural world every day, whether we are there to witness them or not. I wonder just how accurate our descriptions are of the lives of our animal neighbors, after all we only see what they want us to see. I wonder what they are doing when we aren't looking.

ABOUT THE AUTHOR

Barb Barton is a Michigan based singer/songwriter, guitarist, author, wild foods forager, and endangered species biologist. She lives her life seeking adventures and trying to make the world a better place for the next generations. Although she has had many wonderful adventures in her lifetime, the backstory is a life-long struggle with depression. Her iron will and determination to live a good life has carried her through poverty, homelessness, and addiction. She has transformed all those challenges into a full life and tries to help others do the same.

Barton is also the author of *Manoomin: The Story of Wild Rice in Michigan*, published by Michigan State University Press (June 2018).